PIVOTAL
MOMENTS
IN HISTORY

THE SPANISH
CONQUEST OF MEXICO

SYLVIA A. JOHNSON

TFCB

TWENTY-FIRST CENTURY BOOKS
MINNEAPOLIS

Consultant: John Bierhorst, translator and editor of *The Hungry Woman, Myths and Legends of the Aztecs* (William Morrow, 1984) and *Cantares Mexicanos: Songs of the Aztecs* (Stanford University Press, 1985).

Primary source material in this text is printed over an antique-paper texture.

This illustration from the Lienzo de Tlaxcala *shows a battle scene between Spanish and indigenous forces during the Spanish conquest of Mexico in the 1500s.*

Twenty-First Century Books
A division of Lerner Publishing Group, Inc.
241 First Avenue North
Minneapolis, MN 55401 U.S.A.

Website address: www.lernerbooks.com

Library of Congress Cataloging-in-Publication Data

Johnson, Sylvia A.
    The Spanish conquest of Mexico / by Sylvia A. Johnson.
       p.   cm. — (Pivotal moments in history)
    Includes bibliographical references and index.
    ISBN 978–0–8225–9079–8 (lib. bdg. : alk. paper)
    1. Mexico—History—Conquest, 1519–1540—Juvenile literature. I. Title.
F1230.J58 2009
972'.02—dc22   2008022939

Manufactured in the United States of America
1 2 3 4 5 6 – BP – 14 13 12 11 10 09

CONTENTS

CHAPTER ONE
THE WORLD OF THE MEXICA

Thus they have come to tell it, . . .

the ancient men, the ancient women.

They were our grandfathers, our grandmothers, . . .

Their account was repeated,

they left it to us; . . .

to us who live now,

to us who come down from them.

—Crónica Mexicayotl, *a history of the Mexica written in the late 1500s*

On November 8, 1519, two men met on a causeway in a great city in the middle of a lake. One was a king, the ruler of thousands of people. He wore sandals decorated with gold and gems, and not one of his own escorts dared to look him in the eye. The other was a soldier dressed in travel-worn clothes, the confident leader of a small army of men.

The king was Motecuzoma II, ruler of the Mexica (also called Aztec) empire in present-day Mexico, and the great city

Motecuzoma and Hernán Cortés met for the first time in Tenochtitlan on November 8, 1519. This painting is one of eight known as the Conquest of Mexico series. The series was created in the 1600s by unknown artists who were inspired by the Historia de la Conquista de México *(History of the Conquest of Mexico) published by Antonio de Solís in 1684.*

was his capital, Tenochtitlan. The soldier was Hernán Cortés, an explorer and adventurer from faraway Spain. These men came from two different worlds that were meeting for the first time on that November day. The outcome of their meeting would become a pivotal moment in world history, bringing about changes that would affect the lives of millions.

When Motecuzoma and Hernán Cortés met in November 1519, the Mexica were the most powerful people in Mesoamerica, an area that includes most of modern Mexico as well as parts of Guatemala, Honduras, El Salvador, Nicaragua, Costa Rica, and Belize. Their armies controlled a vast territory and exacted tribute from many other native peoples. Their

WHAT'S IN A NAME?

You might be surprised that the word *Aztec* appears only once in a book describing ancient Mexico. This familiar name has been around for years, but most modern scholars use the name *Mexica*, which is the original name of the people later known as the Aztecs. The term *Aztec* was first used by writers during the 1700s. It was derived from Aztlan, the name of the legendary homeland of the Mexica.

capital city was a large metropolis with gleaming temples and bustling markets. But the Mexica were relative newcomers in Mesoamerica. Many other cultures had preceded them.

EARLY CIVILIZATIONS OF MEXICO

As early as 1500 B.C., people in Mesoamerica were living in small settlements and raising crops of maize (corn), beans, squash, and other domesticated plants. The first towns appeared about 1200 B.C., built by the Olmec people along Mexico's Gulf Coast. In later centuries, large cities such as Palenque, Yaxchilan, and Tikal arose in the dense forests of southern Mexico and Guatemala. These were centers of the classic Maya civilization, which lasted from about A.D. 300 to 900. During this period, Maya people developed a sophisticated written language and a number system more precise than the Roman numerals then used in Europe.

During the years that the Maya cities thrived, another important civilization dominated central Mexico, where the

Mexica would later establish their empire. This civilization was centered in the city of Teotihuacan, which had its beginnings around A.D. 300.

The name Teotihuacan came from the Nahuatl language spoken by the Mexica, who saw the ruins of the great city five hundred years after its collapse. They called it the "place of the gods." At the height of its power, Teotihuacan covered an area of about 7 square miles (18 square kilometers) and had a population of about fifty thousand. The people of Teotihuacan produced pottery and made tools out of the volcanic rock obsidian. These items were traded widely, and the city's influence was felt all over Mesoamerica.

Teotihuacan declined after A.D. 600 and finally collapsed around A.D. 700, destroyed either by internal conflict or

HOW DO YOU SAY THAT?

Words in Nahuatl, the language of the Mexica, may look complicated, but the rules for pronouncing them are fairly simple. The letter *x* is pronounced like *sh*, as in meh-SHEE-kah. *Hu* sounds like *hw*, and *tl* is pronounced as in the words *atlas* or *Atlantic*. An example: the name of the god Huitzilopochtli is pronounced hweet-sih-luh-POCH-tlee. When *tl* comes at the end of a word, the *l* is hardly pronounced, as in NAH-hwat(l). There are a few other letter combinations to watch for: the *qu* in *que* and *qui* sound like *k*. For example, Quetzalcoatl is keht-sahl-KOH-aht(l). *Qua* and *quo* are pronounced like *kw*. *Z* sounds like *s*. In most Nahuatl words, the accent or stress is on the second-to-last syllable.

foreign armies. During the next two hundred years, central Mexico was invaded by various groups of Chichimecs—nomadic, warlike people who came in from the north seeking new land and homes.

A WARRIOR SOCIETY

One group of nomadic Chichimecs, the Toltecs, built the city of Tula around A.D. 900. Even after settling into city life, the Toltecs did not forget their warlike past. They extended their power over central Mexico by military conquest and honored their victorious armies by erecting giant stone figures of fierce warriors in their temples.

Other stone figures of reclining men, called *chacmools*, have been found at Tula and other places where Toltec influence was felt. Archaeologists think the flat plates that the figures hold on their stomachs may have been used to receive the hearts of people sacrificed to the gods.

The Toltecs dominated central Mexico not only by military force but also by economic influence. Like the Teotihuacanos before them, they controlled the obsidian trade in the region. This rock produced by volcanic eruptions could be shaped into cutting tools with very sharp edges. Obsidian and other stone tools were vitally important in a world where metal tools and weapons were virtually unknown.

Toltec power in central Mexico lasted only about two hundred years, but the memory of Toltec military might and of its gods and rulers lived on. Among those who inherited the Toltec legacy were the Mexica people who met Cortés on that November day in 1519.

UNWELCOME STRANGERS

Like the Toltecs, the Mexica seem to have been wandering Chichimec people who came into central Mexico from the north. They made their first appearance in the region about 1200, and the local inhabitants did not welcome the crude and aggressive newcomers. Later, the Mexica remembered how their ancestors were treated: "They were not received anywhere. Everywhere they were reprimanded. . . . Everywhere they said to them, 'Who are you? From where do you come?'" (These lines come from a book known as the *Florentine Codex*, written by a Spanish friar in the 1550s.)

THE *FLORENTINE CODEX*

The *Florentine Codex* is a remarkable historical document. It was created by a Franciscan friar, Bernardino de Sahagún, who came to Mexico in 1529. To aid in his work as a missionary, Sahagún set out to learn all he could about Mexica history, religion, and culture. He enlisted the help of young Mexica men who had already been converted to Christianity and could read and write in Spanish. His assistants interviewed hundreds of Mexica people and wrote down their memories and observations in Nahuatl using the Latin alphabet. Sahagún then translated the material into Spanish. He also commissioned native artists to illustrate the work, which he called *The General History of the Things of New Spain*. Modern historians often refer to it as the *Florentine Codex* because the most complete surviving copy is kept in a library in Florence, Italy.

By the 1200s, many of the settled inhabitants of central Mexico lived in communities located in a large, fertile valley surrounded by mountains. In the center of the valley was a shallow lake known as Lake Texcoco. Cities such as Azcapotzalco, capital of the Tepanec people, and Colhuacan, an ancient kingdom with Toltec origins, were located near the lake.

These established communities were not eager to share their lands and their power with the uncivilized Mexica newcomers. Their leaders, however, were willing to hire the fierce Mexica warriors to fight in wars against other local rulers. While they used their military skills in such battles, the Mexica lived in temporary settlements and continued their search for the home their gods had promised them.

A PLACE TO CALL HOME

The most important god in the Mexica religion was Huitzilopochtli, a war god who had triumphed over other gods, including his own sister and brothers, in a fierce and terrifying battle. According to legend, this powerful deity guided the Mexica people in their journey from the north and told them to look for a special sign. When they saw an eagle with a snake in its mouth perched on a prickly pear cactus, this would be the place to establish their new community.

In 1345 the Mexica finally saw the sign they had been seeking on a rocky island surrounded by marshes near the western shore of Lake Texcoco—"in the middle of the waters, . . . among the reeds and rushes." Here they built their city and named it Tenochtitlan, "the place of the fruit of the cactus."

The Mexica had found a home, but they had not yet achieved the independence that they sought. The island on which they settled was under the control of the Tepanecs of Azcapotzalco. The city's rulers demanded tribute from the inhabitants of Tenochtitlan and recruited their warriors to fight in local wars. It would be more than eighty years before the Mexica could free themselves from Tepanec power.

To strengthen their position in the Valley of Mexico, Mexica leaders established connections

This illustration from the Aubin Codex, a pictorial history created from 1576 to 1607, shows the eagle and cactus that the Mexica saw as signs of their new homeland.

with another important lake city, Colhuacan, whose rulers were descended from the much-admired Toltecs. A Colhua princess married a Mexica leader, and their son, Acamapichtli, became the first king of Tenochtitlan in 1376.

In the Nahuatl language, the Mexica king was called *tlatoani*, which means "speaker," or "he who says something." Skill in making fine speeches was important for Mexica rulers, but a tlatoani also had to be an expert military leader. Marching

The Toltecs were wise. Their works
were all good, all perfect. . . .
The Toltecs were skilled. . . .
They invented all the precious,
marvelous things which they made. . . .
They were thinkers. . . .
So wise were they [that] they understood
the stars that were in the heavens. . . .
The Toltecs were righteous. They were not deceivers.
Their words were clear words. . . .
They were tall; they were larger than the people today.

—*A passage from the* Florentine Codex *describing the Toltecs*

at the head of large armies, early Mexica kings set out to conquer neighboring kingdoms in central Mexico and to make allies of others. In 1428 the tlatoani Itzcoatl finally defeated the Tepanecs of Azcapotzalco. The Mexica strengthened their power in the region by forming a Triple Alliance with two other important cities, Texcoco and Tlacopan. Itzcoatl's successors continued the string of conquests in central Mexico.

By the time of Motecuzoma I, who was tlatoani from 1440 to 1469, the Mexica controlled large parts of Mesoamerica. When his great-grandson Motecuzoma II took the throne in 1502, he ruled an empire that stretched for thousands of miles, from the Gulf of Mexico in the north to the Pacific Ocean in the south. The Mexica were masters of their world, but they had made many enemies in their march to power.

THE GREAT CITY

When Motecuzoma II became tlatoani, the Mexica capital, Tenochtitlan, was less than 150 years old. The first crude settlement on the island in Lake Texcoco had grown into a city unequalled in size and splendor, not only in Mesoamerica but also in most of Europe and Asia.

From that one small island, the city had spread to include other nearby islands, sandbanks, and marshes in the lake. These land areas had been built up with soil taken from the shore or the lake bottom and were joined together by causeways and bridges. Canals and water channels threaded through Tenochtitlan, similar to the watery streets in Venice, Italy.

This map, based on a sketch sent by Cortés to the Spanish king Charles I in 1520, shows Tenochtitlan in Lake Texcoco. Causeways connect the city to the mainland. The body of water on the left depicts the Gulf of Mexico. The artist added European-style architecture and other creative details to the map when it was included in a published work in 1524.

In the early 1500s, the Mexica capital covered an area of about 6 or 7 square miles (16 to 18 sq. km) and had a population of about two hundred thousand. (Some modern historians think five hundred thousand may have lived there.)

At the heart of this splendid city was a large central square. Twin temples to Huitzilopochtli and Tlaloc, the god of rain, were perched on top of a tall pyramid that towered over the square. On another side was the emperor's palace, a two-story building made of whitewashed stone that contained dozens of luxuriously decorated rooms. Also on the main square were other palaces of Mexica nobles, as well as government buildings and temples dedicated to important gods such as Quetzalcoatl the Feathered Serpent and the sky god Tezcatlipoca.

From Tenochtitlan's central square, four main roads stretched out in four directions. These roads divided the city into four quarters where the *macehualtin*, the common Mexica people, lived and worked.

FARMERS AND CRAFTSPEOPLE

The macehualtin provided the broad base on which the Mexica empire was built. The food they grew, the products they made, and the roads and buildings they constructed made possible the bustling life of Tenochtitlan. As foot soldiers in the tlatoani's armies, the macehualtin also played a major role in the conquests that had made the Mexica so powerful.

The Mexica records that have survived contain little specific information about the lives of the common people, but modern historians have used the available evidence to put together a general picture. According to these experts,

the macehualtin in Tenochtitlan probably lived in units called *calpultin*. Each *calpulli* was made up of groups of families who shared an area of land in one of the city's four quarters. Families made their homes in simple, one-story houses constructed of adobe. Often all the members of an extended family lived in a compound that consisted of a central courtyard surrounded by houses.

If families lived on the outskirts of Tenochtitlan, they usually had a small plot of land where they could raise vegetables for their own use and for sale in the city markets. Some farmed on *chinampas*, pieces of land created by piling dirt onto platforms of logs, branches, and reeds that floated in the lake. In other areas

This mural, painted in the 1960s, is on display at the Museo de la Ciudad de Mexico in Mexico City. Based on a sixteenth-century manuscript, it shows the Mexica building chinampas for agriculture.

of the city, members of a calpulli might be craftspeople who produced clothing, pottery, stone tools, or other useful items.

The skilled workers who made fine gold jewelry or wove cloaks of brightly colored feathers had their own special districts. The *Florentine Codex* says that these artisans were called Toltecs because their artistic creations were inspired by the great Toltec civilization.

As citizens of Tenochtitlan, the craftspeople, small farmers, and other ordinary Mexica supported the central government by paying taxes. These were in the form of goods and services, since ancient Mexico did not have a monetary system. Unskilled workers from the calpultin were assigned to maintain roads and canals and to build new temples and palaces. The Toltecs and other skilled craftspeople contributed their products to the tax system. Pottery, tools, clothing, and fine pieces of jewelry were sent to the central government to be used by the ruler and nobles or added to the state treasury.

In return for their labor, ordinary Mexica living in Tenochtitlan received certain benefits from the state. Their children could attend state-run schools where they learned the skills needed in their daily lives. In times when food was scarce, the common people received supplies of maize and other produce from the government stores.

Like ordinary people in most European societies in the early 1500s, the macehualtin had few rights. They had no role in choosing their ruler or in making decisions about the actions of the central government. Their everyday lives were simple. Ordinary people seldom ate meat. Their diet was based on maize, beans, peppers, and squash. Their clothing—cloaks, skirts, capes, and loincloths—was not made of soft cotton like the garments of the nobles but of rough cloth woven from the fiber of the agave plant. They were forbidden to wear sandals. This privilege was kept for the upper classes.

Despite these limitations, the common people actively participated in Tenochtitlan's many religious ceremonies and festivals. The men marched proudly behind the great warriors into battles against the enemies of Tenochtitlan. If he proved himself in battle, a young man from the macehualtin class could rise within the army to become a military leader. The common Mexica people lived by strict social rules, as did other members of Mexica society, but they could improve their lives.

MERCHANTS AND TRADERS

Above the common people on the Mexica social ladder were the *pochteca*, merchants and traders who played a unique role in Mexica society. Trade and commerce were very important in the life of the Mexica empire. The large public market located in Tlatelolco, the city immediately north of Tenochtitlan, was a busy, bustling place, with hundreds of vendors selling all kind of goods. Some displayed varieties of maize, beans, peppers, amaranth seeds, and other farm produce. Others offered cooked food such as tamales or tortillas in many forms: "With shelled beans mashed, . . . wrapped with chilli [peppers], . . . with turkey eggs." In a different part of the market, pottery, cloth, tools, rope, leather goods, and other useful products were sold. Shoppers bartered for their purchases or used cacao beans and lengths of cloth as forms of trade currency.

The pochteca usually did not offer their wares in the Tlatelolco market. Their specialty was foreign trade. These merchants made long journeys to cities and towns far from Tenochtitlan. They carried with them products made in the city, such as clothing, blankets, gold jewelry, and stone knives. On the return journey, they brought back exotic raw materials— seashells and tortoiseshells, jade and emeralds, and spotted jaguar skins and brilliantly colored bird feathers. These materials were used to make the luxurious clothing and ornaments prized by the emperor and the upper classes and used in religious ceremonies.

The pochteca did not have easy lives. During their travels, the merchants often had to defend themselves from hostile tribes that were not part of the Mexica empire. In reporting to the emperor about their work, they said, "We have risked our heads and our lives, and we have labored day and night." Hardworking merchants were rewarded, however. Unlike the ordinary citizens of Tenochtitlan, they could accumulate wealth and keep it. They didn't have to trade their wealth for fine clothing or elaborate feasts, as the nobles of the city were obliged to do. Most pochteca wore plain, even tattered, clothes and lived in modest homes. They kept to themselves, living in a separate district in the city and worshipping their own special gods.

WARRIORS AND NOBLES

Near the top of Mexica society was a class of privileged people who had great power and influence. Because warfare was so vital to the Mexica, some of these important men were military leaders. Others were members of noble families. On a lower rung of the social ladder were the judges and officials who ran the empire's government.

The military leaders in the Mexica upper class were usually warriors who had had long and distinguished military careers. They had fought many battles and had brought home hundreds of war captives to be sacrificed to the Mexica gods. A young soldier was not considered a real warrior until he had taken his first captives. As a sign of this achievement, a long lock of hair that he had worn as a boy was cut off. If a warrior continued to prove himself, he might eventually become an Eagle Knight or a Jaguar Knight, one of the elite professional soldiers of the Mexica army.

A terra-cotta Eagle Knight from around 1480

The top "generals" in the army and the most important military leaders in Mexica society usually came from the class of important people called *pipiltin*. In the early 1500s, the pipiltin, unlike the common Mexica people, were able to own land. They had large estates, often given to them by the emperor, and these estates could be passed down from one generation to the next.

The children of the pipiltin class attended a special school called a *calmecac*, which was not usually open to the common people. Here they were taught to read and

A panel from the Florentine Codex *shows children of noble birth attending school.*

write and to speak well. Students also studied religion and learned to recite the songs and stories that told of the Mexica past. The discipline at this school was very harsh, with fasting and bathing in cold water a part of the daily schedule. A calmecac was often called the House of Tears.

Some of the young people who attended the calmecac went on to become priests and priestesses who spent their lives worshipping the gods and participating in religious ceremonies. Others became military leaders or government administrators who were in charge of collecting taxes, building roads, and overseeing the many other jobs that kept the empire running. A few achieved even more important positions, serving directly under the tlatoani.

THE EMPEROR AND HIS ADVISERS

Although the tlatoani was an absolute ruler, he had help in governing his realm. Councillors and advisers assisted him in planning wars and making other important decisions.

In the early 1500s, the ruler's chief adviser was the *cihuacoatl*, who held a position something like that of a vice president in a modern government. When the tlatoani left Tenochtitlan, the cihuacoatl took over as head of the government. This official held such a high position that he alone was allowed to wear sandals in the presence of the emperor.

In addition to the cihuacoatl, the tlatoani had four other advisers. These men were important military leaders and, like the cihuacoatl, were often relatives of the emperor. The Council of Four provided advice in matters of warfare and also played leading roles in the civil government.

It was from this small group of powerful men that a new Mexica ruler was usually chosen. After the death of an old emperor, the council selected one of its own members to rule the empire, with the approval of the chief dignitaries of Tenochtitlan and of its close allies. Motecuzoma II came to the throne in this way. He was a member of the council under the previous emperor and had also proved himself as a military leader. Motecuzoma was considered brave, intelligent, and deeply religious, an ideal candidate for a Mexica ruler.

When Motecuzoma assumed the throne in 1502, he became the most powerful person in the empire and the most privileged. The emperor dressed in fine cotton clothing trimmed with feathers and precious gems. He had hundreds of servants who attended to his every need. But along with great privilege came great responsibility. At his coronation, a Mexica ruler was told, "It is you who will now carry the weight and burden of this state. . . . It is you, lord, . . . [who] are going to sustain this nation."

One of the main responsibilities of the Mexica ruler was to lead the empire. In the early 1500s, this was a complex and difficult job.

THE MEXICA EMPIRE

When Motecuzoma became emperor, the Mexica empire stretched for thousands of miles. Within this large territory were many small states, cities, and towns that had been conquered by Mexica armies. A few independent kingdoms, such as Tlaxcala, had been able to resist Mexica power.

Although the Mexica stationed soldiers throughout the empire, they did not usually create colonies or set up governments in territories under their rule. As long as the conquered people followed the rules laid down by their overlords, they could keep their own leaders, customs, and religions. The main demand that the Mexica made of their subjects was tribute. Each conquered community had to agree to send a supply of specific materials and goods to Tenochtitlan every year.

The variety was incredible. Towns and cities in the hot country near the Gulf Coast sent seashells, tropical fruits, cacao beans, and the feathers of tropical birds such as the quetzal. The long, emerald green tail feathers of the quetzal were highly prized by the Mexica. Cacao was also a valuable commodity. Cacao beans could be processed into *xocolatl*, a tasty drink enjoyed by the Mexica nobility. The beans themselves were sometimes used as a kind of trade currency in the city markets.

Other regions under Mexica control supplied raw materials such as wood, obsidian, gold, and precious gems, while some contributed manufactured products such as shields, jewelry, and cloaks, as well as lengths of woven cloth. Supplies of maize, beans, chili peppers, and other agricultural products also streamed into Tenochtitlan to fill the needs of the Mexica's "tribute empire."

WAS THERE REALLY A MEXICA EMPIRE?

Some modern historians believe that the word *empire* should not be used to describe the political system of the Mexica. This system was different from European empires, such as the Roman Empire. Although the Mexica conquered other people in central Mexico and demanded tribute from them, they did not actually rule the conquered lands. These experts think that their political system might be better described as a loose confederacy, with the Mexica as its most powerful member. The idea that there was a Mexica empire may have come from Europeans such as Hernán Cortés, who used a familiar term to describe a form of government they did not really understand.

Tax collectors supervised the tribute system, sending agents to gather the materials and deliver them to warehouses in Tenochtitlan. From here the goods would be distributed or stored for future use. Some tribute goods would be sent to Texcoco and Tlacopan, the other two members of the Triple Alliance, but most were kept by Tenochtitlan. The common people received a share of food products, especially in times of famine. Gold and precious gems went directly into the storehouses of the emperor and nobles.

Tribute from the conquered peoples of the empire was very important to the Mexica economy. Other areas of Mexica life also depended on the conquests of the armies. Captives taken in warfare had an essential role to play in the all-important Mexica religion.

GODS, PRIESTS, AND SACRIFICE

The Mexica had a complex religion that included the worship of many different gods. When the Mexica arrived in the Valley of Mexico around A.D. 1200, they brought with them the gods that they had worshipped as wandering nomads. Chief among them was Huitzilopochtli, the fierce war god who had guided the Mexica to their new home. This powerful god was also associated with the rising and setting sun. Huitzilopochtli's mother, the earth goddess Coatlicue—She of the Serpent Skirt—was also honored, as was Tezcatlipoca, a god of the night sky whose name means "Smoking Mirror."

In their travels, the Mexica learned about other gods that were worshipped by the more settled people of the valley. One of the most important was Tlaloc, who brought rain and made the crops grow. Another god, Xipe Totec, was associated with fertility and new growth in spring. The ancient deity Quetzalcoatl was a god of the wind but was also associated with agriculture and learning. These gods and many others were adopted by the Mexica and eventually became part of their complex religion. Tenochtitlan was filled with temples dedicated to the various gods and goddesses, and priests conducted ceremonies in their honor at all hours of the day and night.

Priests belonged to a special class in Mexica society. They devoted their lives to the worship of the gods, and most priests did not marry. These religious officials went through many years of training to learn the rituals and ceremonies of the Mexica religion. Many of these ceremonies included the sacrifice of human lives.

Other peoples in ancient Mesoamerica such as the Maya and the Toltecs had made human sacrifices. Ancient societies in Europe, Asia, and Africa also had this practice. Among the Mexica, however, human sacrifice became a basic part of religious life.

According to Mexica legends, the gods had created the universe by offering themselves as sacrifices. To preserve the world and all its inhabitants, humans had to follow their example. Without human blood for nourishment, Huitzilopochtli would not be able to rise from the darkness of night and make his way across the daytime sky. The Mexica believed that blood, "the precious water," kept the sun in its place and Earth and its inhabitants alive. No less important offering could satisfy this need.

In the most common form of sacrifice to Huitzilopochtli, black-robed priests seized a victim and stretched his body over the sacrificial stone in front of the great temple in Tenochtitlan. While four priests held the victim's arms and legs, another would use a sharp flint knife to cut open the chest and rip out the heart while the victim was still alive. The priest lifted up the still-beating heart as an offering to the god and then burned it. They disposed of the victim's body by throwing it down the steps of the temple. The arms and legs were often given to some of the nobles, who cooked and ate pieces of the flesh. They did this so that they could participate in the sacred offering.

Human sacrifice to other gods took different forms. Children were killed to honor the rain god Tlaloc. Their tears were supposed to bring rain in times of drought. Another kind of sacrifices was held in honor of the fertility

A priest performs ritual sacrifices to Huitzilopochtli in this illustration from the Magliabecchi Codex *from the 1600s.*

god Xipe Totec (Our Lord the Flayed One). A victim tied to a frame was first shot with arrows so that his blood dripped down on the earth, symbolizing falling rain. Then a priest removed, or flayed, the skin from the body and put it on as a kind of garment. He danced in this costume to represent the new growth of spring rising out of dead and rotting plants.

Some of the people sacrificed during these frequent and all-important religious ceremonies were slaves who were bought in Tenochtitlan's markets. The majority, however, were war captives. During a battle, Mexica warriors tried to capture rather than kill enemy soldiers, so that they could be brought back to Tenochtitlan. The armies also took captives from the civilian populations of the territories they conquered.

During the important yearly religious festivals and at events such as a ruler's coronation, hundreds or even thousands of victims were offered on the altars of Tenochtitlan. It soon became difficult to fill the ever-growing demand for human lives. To solve this problem, the Mexica and some of their neighbors created a new kind of warfare, known as Flower Wars.

Flower Wars, which began during the late 1400s, were designed not to defeat an enemy but only to take captives. Participants in this kind of warfare often planned their conflicts in advance, agreeing to meet on the field of battle at a specified day and time. Rather than assaults by troops of soldiers, a Flower War involved hand-to-hand combat between powerful warriors who tried to take one another prisoner. Both sides expected to lose some of their men in these wars.

THE MEXICA WORLD IN 1519

In the early 1500s, the Mexica had come a long way from their humble beginnings as a wandering tribe. As rulers of an empire, they had to deal with many political and economic issues that affected the future of the Mexica state. Once members of a single tribe, the Mexica people had become divided into social classes with different degrees of wealth and power. Religion united the Mexica but also placed a heavy burden on their lives.

In November 1519, when Motecuzoma II met the Spaniard Hernán Cortés in Tenochtitlan, new forces were set in motion that would remake the Mexica world completely.

CHAPTER TWO

THE SPANISH WORLD

Most Christian, exalted, excellent, and powerful princes,
King and Queen of the Spains. . . . It was in this year of
1492 that Your Highnesses concluded the war against
the Moors [North Africans] who reigned in Europe. . . .
Afterwards, in that same [year], . . . Your Highnesses
decided to send me, Christopher Columbus, to the regions
of India, to see . . . the people and the lands, and to learn
of their disposition, . . . and the measures which could be
taken for their conversion to our Holy Faith.

—The Log of Christopher Columbus, *1492*

Hernán Cortés came from a world far removed from
Motecuzoma's empire in Mexico. Separated by thousands of
miles of ocean, Spain and Mexico were very different in their
geography and the culture and religion of their inhabitants.
What the two regions did have in common was a past filled
with conflict and a continuing struggle for power.

The Iberian Peninsula, where Spain is located, is the
part of Europe that extends farthest west into the Atlantic

Ocean. The great rock of Gibraltar guards the narrow strait that separates the Atlantic from the Mediterranean Sea, around which many early civilizations developed.

The peninsula was named for the Iberian people, who settled in the area around 2000 B.C. In later years, other civilizations found their way to this land on the edge of the known world. The Phoenicians and the Greeks established trading settlements on the coasts but did not venture into the interior of the peninsula.

Around 250 B.C., Carthage, a powerful Phoenician city in North Africa, conquered most of the Iberian Peninsula. Under the leadership of a skillful general named Hannibal, the Carthaginians fought a long war with Rome. They were eventually defeated in 201 B.C., and the Iberian Peninsula became part of the Roman world.

United by Roman law and the Latin language, the Iberian Peninsula prospered. The territory that the Romans called Hispania was rich in silver and copper and also produced olive oil for the lamps and cooking pots of Rome. During the early A.D. 100s, Roman cities such as Toledo and Córdoba became centers of trade and culture.

When barbarian tribes from the north invaded the Roman Empire beginning in the early 400s, the Iberian Peninsula came under the control of the Visigoths, a tribe from the Germanic lands. Roman Spain became a Visigoth kingdom, ruled by Christian kings who spoke a Germanic language. But Latin remained the language of the people and eventually developed into modern Spanish and Portuguese.

The Visigoth kingdom survived until the early 700s, when it fell before a new invader. In 711 Moorish armies from

North Africa swept into the Iberian Peninsula. They brought with them the religion of Islam, which had been founded in Arabia less than one hundred years earlier. North African people known as Moors took over most of the peninsula and established kingdoms that would dominate the region for five hundred years. They named their new land al-Andalus.

MOORISH SPAIN

During the early Middle Ages (around A.D. 1000), al-Andalus was one of the most civilized areas in a Europe still recovering from the dark ages that followed the collapse of the Roman Empire. Under Moorish rule, the old Roman cities of Córdoba and Toledo became centers of learning where the writings of Aristotle and other Greek philosophers were studied and translated. Scholars in Muslim Spain wrote treatises on medicine and made accurate observations of the stars. Students from many parts of the world came to study with these learned men.

Not all the inhabitants of the Muslim kingdoms were followers of Islam. Many Christians and Jews also lived in the Moorish cities. Because they had their own sacred scriptures similar to the Quran, they were considered "People of the Book." As such, Jews and Christians were allowed to practice their own religions, although their rights were strictly limited. Jews, in particular, found a welcome refuge in Muslim Spain, where persecution was less common than in the rest of Europe.

Although the Moors ruled most of Spain for centuries, they never conquered the far northern part of the Iberian Peninsula. In this region, small Christian kingdoms grew up in the 900s and 1000s. As their rulers became more powerful, they began to send their armies south to attack the cities of Muslim Spain. This was the beginning of La Reconquista, the Christian reconquest of Spain.

In 1085 the city of Toledo fell to Christian forces. Córdoba was overrun in 1236, and Seville, in 1248. The only Muslim kingdom left undefeated was Granada, which maintained its power for another two hundred years.

An illuminated Spanish manuscript from the 1200s pictures a battle between Christian and Moorish forces during the reconquest of Spain.

The final defeat of the Moors came about because the forces of Christian Spain were united under the leadership of two powerful rulers. Queen Isabella of Castile and her husband, King Ferdinand of Aragon, led other Christian princes in the assault against Granada, which lasted from 1481 to 1492.

When Granada surrendered in January 1492, the Italian navigator Christopher Columbus was there to witness the final defeat of Moorish Spain. "In the great city of Granada, I saw the royal banners of Your Highnesses [Isabella and Ferdinand] placed by force of arms on the towers of the Alhambra, which is the fortress of the city." After almost eight centuries of conflict, La Reconquista was complete.

THE CATHOLIC MONARCHS

After La Reconquista, Isabella and Ferdinand set out to unite Spain under their leadership. As part of their plan, the monarchs established relations with the new towns and cities that were appearing in Spain. Officials in these towns would deal directly with the king and queen rather than with a local landlord or nobleman.

Isabella and Ferdinand also wanted to unite their realm by eliminating the religious diversity that had existed in Muslim Spain. Roman Catholic Christianity would be the only religion of the Spanish people.

The monarchs concentrated their efforts on the Spanish Jews. In the early 1400s, thousands of Jews living in the Christian kingdoms had been forced to convert to Christianity. Spanish church and government officials often looked on these conversos and their descendants with suspicion. To deal with the problem, the Holy Office of the Inquistion was established in the 1480s. Conversos suspected of being false Christians were brought before the judges of the Inquisition and questioned about their beliefs. If converted Jews failed to pass the test, they could be imprisoned or executed.

The Inquisition had no jurisdiction over Jews who had not converted. But these people did not fit into the unified Christian Spain that Isabella and Ferdinand hoped to create. In March 1492, the two monarchs issued an Edict of Expulsion ordering all Jews to leave Spain within three months. Leaving most of their property behind, the Spanish Jews fled to Portugal, France, and North Africa.

Both the conquest of Granada and the expulsion of the Jews took place in the crucial year 1492. Another event in that year would have an impact far beyond Spain's borders. In 1492 Christopher Columbus left the Spanish port of Palos and set out on a momentous voyage of discovery.

Up until this time, Portugal, Spain's smaller neighbor on the Iberian Peninsula, had been the leader in European exploration. Seeking a route to the rare spices, jewels, and other riches of the East, Portuguese navigators had gradually made their way down the west coast of Africa and across the Indian Ocean to India.

Like the Portuguese explorers, Christopher Columbus also wanted to find a route to China, Japan, and the fabulous Spice Islands of the Indies. Like all educated people of his day, Columbus knew that Earth was round. He reasoned that if a ship sailed west across the Atlantic Ocean, it would eventually reach the lands of spice and treasure. According to his estimates, the distance between Europe and the East was only about 3,550 miles (5,680 km).

In 1484 King John II of Portugal had refused to sponsor Columbus's voyage, insisting that his estimates were completely wrong. (Columbus's figures were wrong, of course. More than 11,000 miles [17,700 km] separate Europe and Asia, not to mention a whole other continent.)

Undiscouraged, Columbus had gone to Spain to present his ideas to Queen Isabella and King Ferdinand. In 1492, after the fall of Granada, Isabella and Ferdinand were finally ready to turn their attention to the world outside of Spain. They agreed to help finance Columbus's voyage of exploration.

The goals of Columbus's expedition would be both material and spiritual. The Spanish monarchs hoped to find new trade routes to the East that would bring wealth and profit to Spain. "As Catholic Christians and Princes devoted to the Holy Christian faith," they also wanted to convert the heathen people of other worlds to Christianity.

On August 3, 1492, Columbus's three small ships, the *Niña*, *Pinta*, and *Santa Maria*, left Spain, sailing under the flags of Aragon and Castile. The voyage across the Atlantic took three long months, and it did not end in the East Indies or Japan. Instead, Christopher Columbus found another world unknown to Europe. On October 12, 1492, Columbus landed on a small island in the Bahamas that he named San Salvador, "in honor of Our Blessed Lord." The explorer unfurled the royal banners and claimed the new land for Isabella and Ferdinand. Spain had arrived in the New World.

SPANISH COLONIES IN THE CARIBBEAN

Christopher Columbus was convinced that he had reached the East Indies, but other explorers who followed him

"At dawn . . . , I went ashore in the ship's boat. . . . I unfurled the royal banner and the captains brought the flags which displayed a large green cross with the letters F [Ferdinand] and Y [Isabella] at the left and the right side. . . . After a prayer of thanksgiving, I ordered the captains of the *Pinta* and *Niña* . . . to bear faith and witness that I was taking possession of this island for the King and Queen."

—The Log of Christopher Columbus, 1492

realized his mistake. Still, they hoped to find something of value in this new world. On San Salvador, Columbus had seen "a few natives who wear a little piece of gold hanging from a hole in the nose," but the precious metal was scarce in the islands and difficult to find.

The Caribbean islands also lacked exotic spices such as cinnamon and pepper, which were valued products of the East. Columbus did see some amazing plants growing on the islands, however, "as different from ours as day is from night." There were orange sweet potatoes, spicy red peppers, and tall maize plants. These new lands were not the East Indies, but they might still prove profitable for the Spanish crown.

The islands of the Caribbean might also provide a fertile field for Christian missionaries. When Columbus met the native people of San Salvador, he described them as "friendly and well-dispositioned" and thought that they "could easily be made Christians, for they seem to have no religion." Columbus also noted that they learned quickly and should make "good and skilled servants."

Not long after Columbus's discoveries, permanent settlements began to appear in Isabella and Ferdinand's new realm. In 1502 a fleet of ships brought twenty-five hundred men and women to settle on La Isla Española ("the Spanish Island," later known as Hispaniola). Santo Domingo became a major city on the island, and smaller communities of farmers and tradespeople were established. But some of those who came to Hispaniola were not interested in settling down. They were young men seeking fortune and adventure in a world where possibilities seemed endless.

A CHAPTER THREE
NEW WORLD

Two ways were open to [Cortés] at this time, both of which suited his purpose and inclination: one, to go to Naples . . . ; the other, to go to the Indies. . . . Hernán Cortés was nineteen when he went to the Indies in the year of Our Lord 1504 and as young as he was he dared to make this long voyage alone.

—*Francisco López de Gómara*, Cortés: The Life of the Conqueror, 1552

Hernán Cortés was one of those young men who came to make their fortunes in the New World. Cortés was born in 1485 in the small town of Medellin, in the province of Extremadura, a rugged region in southern Spain.

Hernán's father, Martín, was a hidalgo (a minor nobleman) and his mother, Catalina, was also from this class. Despite their position, the family was not wealthy. Martín Cortés, like so many men of his rank, had fought in the wars against the Moors and may even have taken part in the final assault on Granada. His son no doubt heard stories of the great wars and the brave Christian soldiers who had proved themselves in battle against the Muslims. The Moorish wars were over, however, and opportunities to achieve military glory were limited.

Not much is known about Hernán Cortés's early years. He certainly had a basic education and learned to read and write in Castilian, the dialect of Spanish spoken in Extremadura. As a young man, Hernán spent some time in the city of Salamanca, where a noted Spanish university was located. There are no records of his attending the university, although he may have learned some Latin while living in Salamanca. Latin was the language of scholars and used in schools all over Europe.

Other accounts of Cortés's early life report that he worked for a notary in the town of Valladolid, where he learned to write contracts, wills, and other legal documents. Cortés did have these skills and used them later in his career. But such dull work did not seem to suit his personality. Francisco López de Gómara said of him: "He was restless, haughty, mischievous, and given to quarreling, for which reason he decided to seek his fortune."

In 1501 Cortés planned to join an expedition leaving for the West Indies, but an injury prevented him from making the voyage. (According to López de Gómara, he fell from a wall while climbing into or out of a lady's window.) It was not until 1504 that Hernán Cortés left Spain to begin his great adventure, sailing on a ship headed for the island of Hispaniola.

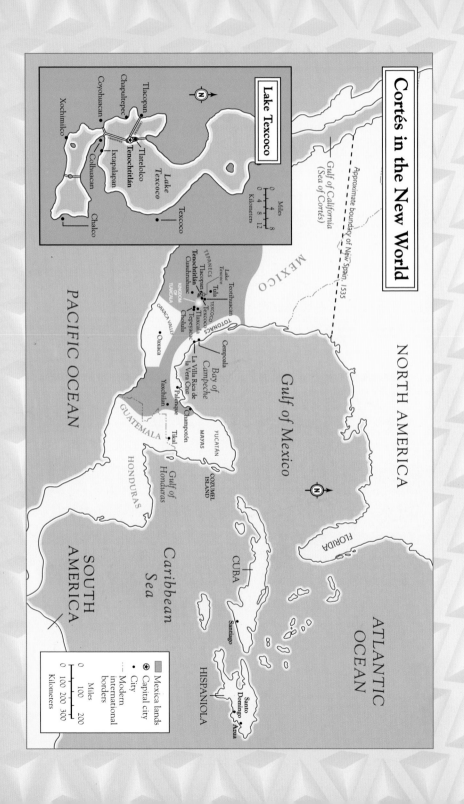

Cortés in the New World

NORTH AMERICA

MEXICO

Approximate boundary of New Spain, 1535

Gulf of California (Sea of Cortés)

PACIFIC OCEAN

Gulf of Mexico

TEPANECS
Lake Texcoco
Tlacopan
Tenochtitlan
Cuauhnahuac
Tula
Teotihuacan
TEXCOCO
Texcoco
Tlaxcala
Tepeyacac
Cholula
KINGDOM OF TLAXCALA

OAXACA VALLEY

Oaxaca

TOTONACS

Cempoala
Bay of Campeche
La Villa Rica de la Vera Cruz

Yaxchilan
Palenque
Champotón
Tikal

GUATEMALA

HONDURAS

Gulf of Honduras

YUCATAN

MAYAS

COZUMEL ISLAND

FLORIDA

CUBA

Caribbean Sea

Santiago

HISPANIOLA

Santo Domingo
Azua

SOUTH AMERICA

ATLANTIC OCEAN

Mexica lands
● Capital city
• City
--- Modern international borders

Miles
0   100   200
Kilometers
0 100 200 300

Lake Texcoco

Xochimilco
Coyohuacan
Chapultepec
Tlacopan
Colhuacan
Ixtapalapan
Tlatelolco
Tenochtitlan
Texcoco
Chalco

Lake Texcoco

Miles
0   4   8
Kilometers
0 4 8 12

CORTÉS IN THE NEW WORLD

When Cortés arrived in Hispaniola, he did not find the land of opportunity he was seeking. After twelve years of Spanish occupation, the island was in shambles. The lives of the "friendly and well-dispositioned" Taino people had been virtually destroyed. Instead of raising crops of maize and beans, they were working as slave laborers on Spanish plantations or panning for gold in the island's streams. The Taino had also been infected with European diseases such as smallpox, and their population was drastically reduced.

The Spanish settlers on Hispaniola had not made a great success of their new lives. They fought with one another over possession of land and the right to use native labor. Nicolas Ovando, who had become governor of Hispaniola

DESTRUCTION OF THE INDIES

The devastation in Hispaniola was recorded by Bartolomé de Las Casas, a Spanish priest who strongly criticized his countrymen's treatment of the native people. In his book *A Short Account of the Destruction of the Indies*, Las Casas described the wars waged against the inhabitants of Hispaniola and the murder and torture of anyone who resisted Spanish rule. "The reason that the Christians have murdered on such a vast scale," Las Casas wrote, "is purely and simply greed. They have set out to line their pockets with gold. . . . Their insatiable greed and overweening ambition know no bounds."

in 1500, tried to bring some order to the colony. He crushed native revolts and created towns that would serve as the basis of local Spanish government.

Governor Ovando was a native of the province of Extremadura, and when Cortés arrived, he sought out his countryman. Ovando found work for him to do. Cortés served as a notary in the town of Azua and was also employed at a sugar mill. But he wanted more. When a military official, Diego Velásquez, set out on an expedition to invade the large island of Cuba in 1511, Cortés joined him.

After a brutal massacre of native forces, Velásquez conquered Cuba and established a colony there. He was appointed governor of the island, and Cortés became his secretary. Velásquez also granted Cortés an *encomienda*. This grant entitled him to use the labor of a certain number of native people living in a specific area.

In the eight years that Cortés spent in Cuba, he quarreled frequently with Velásquez over personal and political issues. At one point, the governor put his secretary in jail and threatened to hang him. When he was not fighting with Velásquez, Cortés worked at various jobs. He was a notary and also served as the alcalde (mayor) of Santiago, the Cuban capital. He owned a hacienda (ranch) and had herds of sheep and cattle.

Diego Velásquez sailed to Hispaniola in 1493 on Columbus's second voyage. In 1511 he conquered Cuba.

Like many settlers in Spanish America, Cortés had never given up the search for gold. He used the native workers assigned to him in his encomienda to pan for the precious metal in Cuba's rivers and streams. The gold they recovered, combined with the income from Cortés's other interests, allowed him to live comfortably. But he did not have the wealth he desired.

In Cuba, Cortés became known as a capable, ambitious man who was good with words. He liked to talk and was skillful in persuading others to agree with him. Cortés also had the reputation of "being excessively under the influence of women," both before and after his marriage in 1515 to Catalina Suárez, who had come to Cuba with her brother. Cortés was a devout Catholic but always kept his mind focused on his own earthly goals and ambitions.

Cortés soon found an ideal opportunity to pursue those goals. In 1518 Juan de Grijalva, Governor Velásquez's nephew, had set out on an expedition heading west from Cuba. When Grijalva did not return, Velásquez decided to send out another group to search for him. The governor selected Cortés to be its leader.

ON THE TRAIL OF GRIJALVA

Juan de Grijalva was not the first Spanish explorer who had left the islands of the Caribbean in search of new lands. In 1517 an expedition led by Francisco Hernández de Córdoba had reached the coast of Mexico's Yucatán Peninsula. The explorers met the local Maya people and were impressed by their stone buildings and the gold ornaments they wore. Friendly at first, the Maya eventually attacked the Spaniards, and Córdoba fled back to Cuba. When Governor Velásquez heard about the new discoveries, he immediately organized another expedition to be led by his nephew Juan de Grijalva.

In January 1518, the Grijalva expedition had left Cuba with two hundred men and four small ships. The captain of one of the ships was Pedro de Alvarado, a young man well known in Cuba and Hispaniola for his bravery and cruelty. Another member of Grijalva's crew was a young soldier

The 1684 work, Historia de la Conquista de México, *by Antonio de Solís inspired this painting of Juan de Grijalva landing in Champotón and meeting the Totonacs. Solís based his work on the writings of López de Gómara, Bernal Díaz del Castillo, and Cortés.*

named Bernal Díaz del Castillo, who would later write a famous account of his adventures in the New World.

Grijalva and his men sailed along the coast of the Yucatán Peninsula until they reached the town of Champotón, where Córdoba's expedition had been attacked. Grijalva also met with resistance from the local Maya people and continued along the coast, stopping frequently to explore. Finally, the expedition reached the Gulf Coast of Mexico, where the Totonacs lived.

The Totonac lands were part of the Mexica empire. Their inhabitants sent loads of fine cotton clothing to Tenochtitlan every year as tribute. Resentful of Mexica power, the Totonacs welcomed the Spanish explorers. Perhaps they hoped that these strangers would help to win their freedom.

While exploring Totonac territory, Grijalva and his men saw many prosperous towns and villages. In one of the settlements, Bernal Díaz said that they came upon a temple with "idols with evil looking bodies" and saw "five Indians [who] had been sacrificed before them; their chests had been cut open, and the arms and thighs had been cut off. . . . At all this we stood greatly amazed." This was the first time that the Spaniards had seen evidence of human sacrifice in Mexico.

As usual, the Spanish visitors asked for gold, and the Totonacs brought "jewelry of low grade gold, worked into various forms." Grijalva wanted more. The Totonacs told him that their overlords, the Mexica, had large supplies of the precious metal. They described the great city of Mexico—Tenochtitlan—and its powerful ruler, Motecuzoma II. The Spaniards were fascinated.

In fact, Motecuzoma himself had already heard about Grijalva and his expedition. Reports had been sent to Tenochtitlan about men who had come from the sea riding on tall towers (the native people of Mexico had never before seen ships with tall sails). The emperor sent his representatives to the land of the Totonacs to find out more about these mysterious strangers.

Motecuzoma's agents met Grijalva at a feast held in his honor. The meeting was peaceful, and at its conclusion, Grijalva told the Mexica that he and his men would return. Motecuzoma's representatives hurried back to Tenochtitlan to report this ominous news to the emperor.

Grijalva was ready to return to Cuba, but members of the expedition urged him to stay and establish a colony in the new lands. He refused, saying that he had been sent only to explore. Since some of his men were sick, Grijalva ordered Alvarado to take them back to Cuba ahead of the main expedition. Alvarado carried with him some of the treasures that they had accumulated.

In July 1518, Alvarado reached Cuba and gave Governor Diego Velásquez an enthusiastic report about the rich Mexica empire. Velásquez was impressed, but he was also concerned about his nephew and the rest of the expedition. He decided to send Cortés to search for the missing men and to learn more about the new territory Grijalva had discovered.

PREPARATION FOR THE JOURNEY

Cortés, at first, did not seem to be a very likely candidate for the job. He had little military experience, and he had never

"As soon as Hernando Cortes had been appointed General [of the expedition] he began to search for all sorts of arms, guns, powder and crossbows. . . . Moreover he began to adorn himself and be more careful of his appearance. . . , and he wore a plume of feathers . . . and a gold chain, and a velvet cloak trimmed with knots of gold, in fact he looked like a gallant and courageous Captain."

—Bernal Díaz del Castillo, late 1500s

led an expedition into hostile territory. He was well known to Governor Velásquez, however, and was considered to be "a diligent, discreet, and valorous man." It also helped that Cortés was willing to share the cost of the expedition with Velásquez and other investors. López de Gómara reported that Cortés, "who had the courage and as well as the desire for it, accepted the partnership, the expense and the command of the expedition."

Cortés made quick preparations for his journey. "He approached his friends and many others to inquire if they would go along, and found three hundred who were willing to do so." To transport the expedition, Cortés bought two small sailing ships—a caravel and a brigantine. He obtained another brigantine from Velásquez and a caravel that Pedro de Alvarado had used on his return voyage to Cuba. Alvarado as well as his ship would join the expedition.

After obtaining ships, Cortés began to stock them with supplies. He bought "arms, artillery, and munitions . . . wine, oil, beans, chickpeas." Velásquez observed Cortés's hurried preparations with some concern. He began to think that his former secretary had more ambitious plans for the expedition than had been agreed on.

When he had selected Cortés to be its leader, the governor had drawn up a complicated document outlining his duties and responsibilities. Cortés was to learn more

In another illustration inspired by Solís's writings, Diego Velázquez (second from right) selects Cortés (far right) to lead the expedition to find Grijalva and explore the new land.

about the native people of Yucatán and introduce them to the true religion of the Catholic faith. He was to claim all the lands he visited for Spain. Some trade with the natives was expected, and the treasures thus obtained would be kept in "a box with three locks." Cortés would have only one of the keys.

Velásquez's document said little about the search for Grijalva, supposedly the main purpose of the voyage. In fact, Grijalva had already returned to Cuba, landing on a remote part of the island around October 1. It is not clear whether Velásquez was aware of this when he and Cortés signed the agreement on October 23. But the governor was becoming more and more reluctant to continue with the expedition.

Fearing that Velásquez would try to stop him from leaving Cuba, Cortés made hasty preparations to depart. The expedition sailed from Santiago on November 18, 1518. After making stops at two other Cuban ports to get more ships, men, and supplies, Hernán Cortés left Cuba behind and headed for Mexico on February 10, 1519. The great adventure had finally begun.

CHAPTER FOUR
CORTÉS IN MEXICO

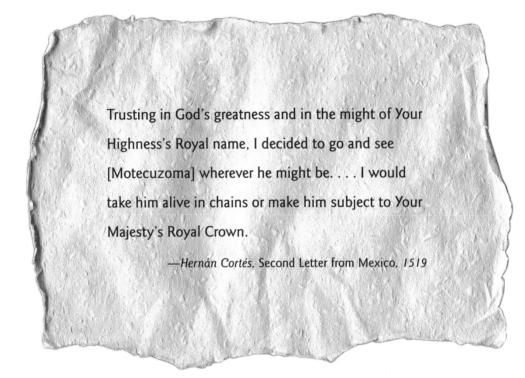

Trusting in God's greatness and in the might of Your
Highness's Royal name, I decided to go and see
[Motecuzoma] wherever he might be. . . . I would
take him alive in chains or make him subject to Your
Majesty's Royal Crown.

—*Hernán Cortés, Second Letter from Mexico, 1519*

Cortés and his expedition reached the mainland of
Mexico in March 1519 after stopping briefly on the island of
Cozumel near the coast of the Yucatán Peninsula. One of the
first challenges Cortés faced was communicating with the
native people. Earlier expeditions had used Maya translators
who had been forced to learn Spanish. Cortés had a different
approach to the problem.

Before leaving Cuba, Cortés had heard stories of two
Spaniards who had been shipwrecked off the coast of

Yucatán in 1511 and captured by the Maya. When he landed on the island of Cozumel, Cortés sent messengers to find these men and pay their captors for their release. Gerónimo de Aguilar was set free, and he eagerly joined Cortés's expedition. The other shipwrecked Spaniard had married a local woman. He was not willing to leave his new life.

Gerónimo de Aguilar was fluent in the Maya language of Yucatán, and he had not forgotten his native Spanish. As Cortés made his way along the coast of the Yucatán Peninsula, following the same route as the Grijalva expedition, Aguilar communicated Cortés's words to the local Maya people.

Like other Spanish explorers, Cortés had a standard proclamation that he delivered to all the native people he encountered. Called the *requerimiento,* or requirement, this was a legal document informing the native leaders that they had to submit to the authority of the Spanish king and the Roman Catholic pope. If they did not do so, they would be punished as traitors. When Cortés came ashore at the large Maya town of Potonchan, Aguilar read out the requerimiento in the local language. The Maya leaders may have understood the words they heard, but the ideas meant nothing to them.

Ignoring the message of the requerimiento, the Maya attacked Cortés and his followers. Bernal Díaz del Castillo described the Maya warriors: "All the men wore great feather crests and they carried drums and trumpets, . . . and they were armed with large bows and arrows, . . . and many slings and fire-hardened [wooden] javelins." The warriors wore protective clothing made out of quilted cotton, but they were no match for Spanish soldiers wielding steel swords and firing cannons.

The biggest threat was the Spanish cavalry. Horses were unknown in Mexico, and the native people were astonished to see these large, fierce animals with men sitting on top of them. The Spanish horsemen attacked with long lances and killed hundreds of Maya soldiers. Cortés lost only thirty-five men and captured the city.

After the defeat of Potonchan, the Maya leaders gave gifts of food, cloth, and gold to the Spanish victors. Also included among the spoils were twenty native women. Giving women to conquerors was a common practice in Mexico. Most of the women were slaves, while some might be noble women who became wives of the victors.

"ONE VERY EXCELLENT WOMAN"

When the twenty captives were handed over to Cortés at Potonchan, he immediately had them baptized in the Roman Catholic faith. One of the women, who was given the Spanish name Marina, would eventually play a significant role in the expedition. In the accounts of Cortés's experiences in Mexico written by Bernal Díaz del Castillo and Francisco López de Gómara, she was usually called by her Spanish name. In other sources, she was called Malintzin, or Malinche. Malinche is the name used by most modern historians.

Malinche's name before she became part of history is unknown. We do know that she came from a region controlled by the Mexica and that she spoke the Mexica language, Nahuatl. When she was a young girl, Malinche was sold as a slave to Maya people living in Yucatán. Growing up among the Maya, she learned their language.

The interpreter Malinche (center) is shown with Cortés (seated) in this illustration from a work by Diego Duran, a Spanish friar. Duran's book, Historia de las Indias de Nueva España *(History of the Indies of New Spain), was written in the 1570s. It recorded the history of the Mexica through the Spanish conquest, including their folktales and beliefs.*

Malinche would become part of a unique translating team. This "very excellent woman," as Díaz described her, would use Nahuatl to talk to the Mexica and other Nahuatl-speaking people whom the expedition encountered. She would then communicate what she had heard to the freed captive Aguilar in the Maya language they both knew, and he would translate her words into Spanish. Cortés used this three-way system of interpretation for many months while Malinche learned Spanish.

MEETING THE MEXICA

The translating team of Malinche and Aguilar was soon put to work when the expedition came into contact with representatives of the Mexica empire. After leaving a defeated Potonchan, Cortés had sailed along the Gulf Coast of Mexico until he reached San Juan de Ulua, the small coastal island where Grijalva had landed. Here the Spanish ships were met by canoes full of native people who spoke Nahuatl. The two translators reported that the men had been sent by Tentlil (or Tendile), a Mexica official in the region. "Their lord, a servant of the great Montezuma [Motecuzoma], had sent them to ask what kind of men we were and of what we were in search."

Soon Tentlil himself appeared to welcome the Spaniards and offer them food and supplies for the camp they had set up on shore. In his book, Bernal Díaz del Castillo described Cortés's meeting with Tentlil. Cortés told the governor that he was a servant of "the greatest lord on earth," the Spanish king Charles I, who had ordered him "to come to this country because for many years he had heard [rumors] about the country and the great prince who ruled it." Cortés expressed his wish to meet the great prince and be friends with him.

Tentlil seemed surprised by this bold speech. He replied, "You have only just now arrived and you already ask to speak with our prince." The Mexica official offered gifts of gold and decorated cloaks and asked Cortés to be patient. In fact, Tentlil had come to learn all he could about the Spaniards. He had brought artists with him, and he "ordered them to make pictures true to nature of the face and body of Cortés and all his captains, and of the soldiers, ships, sails, and horses."

After his meeting with the Spaniards, Tentlil sent messengers to Tenochtitlan with the drawings, made on cloth, and a gilded Spanish helmet that Cortés had offered as a gift. The emperor Motecuzoma was waiting for his report.

Cortés's appearance in Mexico was not completely unexpected. Motecuzoma knew about the earlier Grijalva expedition and the Spaniards' warning that they would return. The foreigners had come back under a new leader, and the emperor faced a difficult situation.

Like all Mexica, Motecuzoma believed in signs and omens that foretold the future. In the years preceding Cortés's appearance, the people of Tenochtitlan had seen some very disturbing signs. The Mexica interviewed in the *Florentine Codex* told of an object "like a flame or tongue of fire . . . throwing off sparks," which appeared frequently in the sky over Tenochtitlan.

This illustration from Diego Duran's work depicts Motecuzoma observing the fiery object in the sky that warned of coming danger.

Other signs were equally disturbing. A fire destroyed the temple of Huitzilopochtli, and the waters of Lake Texcoco boiled. Hunters on the shores of the lake reported seeing a strange bird with a mirror in its head. In the streets of Tenochtitlan, it was said, a woman wandered alone at night, weeping and moaning for her children.

Motecuzoma was alarmed by these omens. He consulted priests and seers, who told him that some unknown danger threatened the land. When the Spaniards arrived on his shores, the emperor's concern grew. Were these pale-skinned strangers ordinary humans, or could they be gods?

THE LEGEND OF QUETZALCOATL

In the Mexica world, the gods took many forms. They were embodied in the sun and the stars and in wind and water. Some gods even showed themselves in human form. Quetzalcoatl was a god of wind and sky, but he was also closely associated with a human.

According to legend, the human Quetzalcoatl had been a ruler or priest in the Toltec city of Tula. His name was Topiltzin, but he also took the name of the god he served. In some stories, Topiltzin Quetzalcoatl was described as a fair-skinned man with a beard. He was a wise leader who cared for his people, but he had enemies. Eventually, these enemies forced him to flee into the east with his followers, but he said that someday he would come back to reclaim his land.

The legend said that Topiltzin Quetzalcoatl left Tula in the year Ce Acatl (One Reed) of the Toltec-Mexica calendar. (The calendar was based on a long cycle, with each year name recurring every fifty-two years.). The year 1519, when Cortés and his men arrived in Mexico, was also Ce Acatl. Was this a coincidence, or could Cortés be the man-god Quetzalcoatl returning as the legends had foretold?

The Mexica considered themselves descendants of the Toltecs, and Motecuzoma was familiar with the story of Quetzalcoatl. The emperor could not be certain of Cortés's

This stone figure from around 1500 shows the god Quetzalcoatl as the Feathered Serpent. He has a snake's body covered by feathers and a man's head. Quetzalcoatl was more closely associated with the Toltec ruler Topiltzin, who promised to return and reclaim his throne.

true identity, but he would treat the Spaniard with caution. If Cortés was a returning god, then he had to be welcomed and honored. If the Spaniard was just another human enemy of the Mexica, Motecuzoma could send an army of thousands to defeat him.

In an effort to deal with both possibilities, Motecuzoma sent the ambassador Tentlil back to the coast with more gifts and a message for Cortés. Díaz reported that one of the gifts was "a wheel like the sun, . . . with many sorts of pictures on it, the whole of fine gold." After presenting this treasure, Tentlil delivered Motecuzoma's message to the strangers: "[The emperor] was pleased that such valiant men . . . should come to his country," but he requested that they stay on the coast, where he would assist them in any way possible.

Cortés replied in his usual smooth style, saying that the Spaniards "had come across so many seas, and had journeyed from such distant lands solely to see and speak with [Motecuzoma] in person. . . . Wherever their prince . . . might be we wished to go and see him." Cortés was determined to go to Tenochtitlan.

THE FOUNDING OF VERA CRUZ

Before Cortés could start his journey to the Mexica capital, he had to deal with problems among expedition members. Some of the men, supporters of Governor Velásquez, claimed that Cortés did not have the authority to stay in Mexico. He needed to go back to Cuba and report to the governor.

Cortés refused to listen to their argument. Instead, with the help of his supporters, he established a town on the Gulf Coast near San Juan de Ulua. He named the settlement La Villa Rica de la Vera Cruz (the Rich City of the True Cross) because it had been founded on Good Friday. Once Vera Cruz was established, Cortés quickly appointed an alcalde and other town officials from among his supporters. These people in turn elected Hernán Cortés as chief justice of the town and captain of the expedition.

In a letter sent to King Charles and his mother, Queen Juana, the officials of Vera Cruz explained their actions: "It seemed to us, . . . that in order to preserve peace and concord amongst ourselves and to govern us well it was necessary to elect someone for Your Royal Service who might act in Your Majesties' name . . . as chief justice, captain and our leader. . . . No person was better fitted for such a responsibility than [Hernán] Cortés."

Since Cortés had been granted authority by the town of Vera Cruz, he no longer needed to follow the orders of Velásquez. In fact, the only people he had to answer to were the king and queen of Spain. Of course, it would take months before their majesties in faraway Spain could approve the actions taken by the Vera Cruz town council. Until then Cortés had no one to answer to but himself.

CORTÉS ON THE MOVE

As Cortés began to move away from the coast toward Tenochtitlan, he soon discovered that all was not well in the Mexica empire. Many of the native people he encountered resented Mexica power and the tribute system that forced them to supply goods to Tenochtitlan. Cortés would use this discontent to bring supporters to his side.

The first people that Cortés enlisted were the Totonacs, who lived in the area near Vera Cruz. (These were the same people who had met Grijalva in 1518.) The leader of the Totonac town of Cempoala expressed his hatred of the Mexica and his willingness to help the Spaniards. According to López de Gómara, he told Cortés that other provinces in the region also were unhappy with Mexica rule. "If Cortés so desired, he would make a league with all of them that would be so strong that Moctezuma [Motecuzoma] would not be able to stand against it." The Totonacs became Cortés's firm allies and supporters, the first of many that he gained in Mexico.

Cortés had acquired a strong native ally, but he was still having problems with his own countrymen. A ship had arrived from Cuba, bringing disturbing news. King Charles had given Cortés's old enemy, Diego Velásquez, the authority to trade with the natives and establish settlements in Mexico. To support his own claims in Mexico, Cortés decided to send the king all the gold and silver that the expedition had collected. (According to Spanish law, the king was entitled to a fifth of the loot.) The treasure ship left for Spain on July 6, 1519, carrying with it a message from Cortés describing the "very great zeal" of his service to the king.

Four days after the ship departed, Cortés faced another setback. Some of Velásquez's supporters planned to leave the expedition and sail back to Cuba. "These men had already got their stores in the ship, . . . and the time being past midnight, were ready to embark" when Cortés discovered the plot. He had the men arrested and sentenced two of them to be hanged. Cortés wrote to the king, "I punished them according to the law and as, in the circumstances, I judged would do Your Majesty greatest service."

Fearing that others would abandon the expedition and return to Cuba, Cortés secretly ordered his captains to disable all the Spanish ships at Vera Cruz. The vessels were stripped of their sails and equipment and dragged up onto the shore. Velásquez's followers protested, but it was too late. The escape route to Cuba was closed, and they had no choice but to follow Cortés to Tenochtitlan.

Back in Cuba, more trouble was brewing for Cortés. The ship carrying the king's gold to Spain had made an unauthorized stop on the island, and Velásquez found out about it. He tried to seize the ship, but it eluded him. Furious, the governor began to organize an expedition that would go to Mexico, capture Cortés, and bring him back to Cuba in chains.

WAR WITH TLAXCALA

Not knowing what Velásquez was planning, Cortés and three hundred of his men left Vera Cruz and began to move inland. With the expedition were some Totonac soldiers and many native porters who carried supplies and equipment, including the heavy Spanish cannons. Along his route, Cortés entered several towns that were loyal to the Mexica. He passed through peacefully, with no resistance from the inhabitants.

As the expedition came closer to Tenochtitlan, Cortés chose a route that would take him through the land of the Tlaxcalans, who were traditional enemies of the Mexica. The rulers of Tlaxcala hated the Mexica, but when the Spaniards appeared in their land, they did not welcome them. Díaz describes the situation: "The whole of Tlaxcala was up in arms against us, for it appears that they had already received news of our approach."

An illustration from Diego Duran's history shows Totonacs carrying the heavy weapons and equipment as the Spaniards move toward Tlaxcala.

Believing that the Spaniards were enemies, the Tlaxcalans attacked them. Díaz gave a vivid account of the battle:

All the plain was swarming with warriors and we stood four hundred men in number. . . . How they began to charge on us! What a hail of stones sped from their slings! . . . The [Tlaxcalan arrows] lay like corn on the threshing floor; all of them barbed and fire-hardened, which would pierce any armour.

The Spaniards and the Tlaxcalans fought several "most perilous and doubtful" battles without either side winning. More than forty-five of Cortés's soldiers were killed, and the rest were wounded, "even with two or three wounds." The Spaniards were also running out of food and other supplies.

On the Tlaxcalan side, many warriors had been killed by Spanish weapons. Finally, Cortés sent several captured warriors to the rulers of Tlaxcala with an offer of peace, along with a threat: "If they did not come to terms, we would slay all their people." The Tlaxcalan leaders accepted the peace offer, although they must have known that the threat was meaningless. The small army of Spaniards would never have been able to kill the thousands of people who lived in the kingdom. Tlaxcala had its own reasons for coming to terms with Cortés.

A NEW ALLY

The Tlaxcalans had seen the power of Spanish firearms and understood what the weapons could do against native armies. By becoming allies of the Spaniards, they hoped to defend themselves against the Mexica empire. With the help of Spanish weapons, it might be even possible to defeat the Mexica and take revenge on these hated enemies.

Representatives of Motecuzoma had been keeping a close eye on Cortés's expedition, and they had informed the emperor about the war in Tlaxcala. Motecuzoma sent "five chieftains, men of much importance," who offered Cortés gifts and advised him not to make a peace agreement with the Tlaxcalans because they could not be trusted. The ambassadors also had another message: Motecuzoma would give the Spaniards tribute in gold and silver if they stayed away from Tenochtitlan. Cortés politely listened to the speeches but ignored the advice.

The Spaniards stayed in Tlaxcala for several weeks, resting and recovering from their wounds. Cortés was impressed with the city, describing it in his second letter as "much larger than Granada and very much stronger with as good buildings and many more people." He and his men were treated well by the Tlaxcalans. Cortés became friendly with two of the city leaders and met with them often. Bernal Díaz del Castillo accompanied Cortés during these meetings and described them in his book.

During his stay in Tlaxcala, Cortés also talked to his new friends about the Catholic religion. Malinche and Aguilar delivered his message, as they had done many times to other native people. (Díaz said that they "were already so expert at it that they explained it very clearly.") Cortés told the Tlaxcalans "that they should at once give up their evil Idols and believe in and worship our Lord God." They also had to stop the terrible practice of human sacrifice.

The Tlaxcalan leaders replied that they "believed . . . this God of yours and this great Lady [the Virgin Mary] are very good," but they could not give up the gods of their ancestors or the sacred ritual of human sacrifice. They did allow the Spaniards to remove the idols from a recently built temple and erect a cross and an image of the Virgin. The Tlaxcalans had no problem adding two more gods to the many they already worshipped.

MASSACRE IN CHOLULA

When Cortés and his expedition left Tlaxcala, they headed for the city of Cholula instead of going directly to Tenochtitlan. The Tlaxcalan rulers had warned the Spaniards not to go this way: the Cholulans were allies and friends of the Mexica. For reasons that are unclear, Cortés did not take their advice. He and his men set out for Cholula, accompanied by five thousand Tlaxcalan warriors.

The leaders of Cholula welcomed the Spaniards and invited them into the city, requesting only that the Tlaxcalan soldiers stay outside. For two days, the Cholulans treated Cortés and his men with hospitality. On the third day, however, they stopped bringing food and would not speak to their guests.

Cortés was immediately on guard. Malinche heard rumors of a planned attack, which she reported to Cortés. "My interpreter, who is an Indian woman . . . , was told by another Indian woman and a native of this city that very close by many of Mutezuma's men were gathered, and that the people of the city had sent away their women and children . . . , and were about to fall on us and kill us all."

On hearing of this supposed plot, Cortés claimed that the people of Cholula had betrayed him. He asked the rulers and nobles of the city to assemble in the courtyard before the temple of Quetzalcoatl. After the group arrived, Spanish soldiers armed with swords blocked the entrances. Díaz was among them. "We were quite prepared for what had to be done," he commented. Cortés accused the Cholulans of treason and said they had to be punished. A musket was fired as a signal, and the Spanish soldiers attacked the group. "We killed many of them, so that they gained nothing from the promises of their false idols."

A native account of the events in Cholula appears in the *Florentine Codex*. According to the people interviewed by Bernardino de Sahagún, the Cholulans had done nothing to provoke Cortés. They had come to the temple courtyard unarmed and were "stealthily and treacherously killed because the Tlaxcalans persuaded [the Spaniards] to do it."

If the Tlaxcalans were behind the attack on Cholula, they gained something by their interference. The Spaniards had defeated a strong ally of the Mexica empire, Tlaxcala's sworn enemy. After the killings in the courtyard, Tlaxcalan warriors entered the city, "plundering and making prisoners. . . . [They] "did great damage," reported Díaz, "for they were very hostile to the people of Cholula." The defeat of Cholula by the Spaniards and their Tlaxcalan friends sent another ominous signal to Motecuzoma. He again dispatched ambassadors to meet with Cortés and persuade him not to come to Tenochtitlan. The emperor also sent priests and soothsayers who used magic to try to stop Cortés. The mission failed on both accounts.

THE ROAD TO TENOCHTITLAN

Hernán Cortés was ready for the final stage of his journey to the Mexica capital. Accompanied by thousands of Tlaxcalan warriors, the expedition left Cholula. Cortés decided on a southern route through the mountains, perhaps at the urging of his Tlaxcalan advisers. As the expedition approached a mountain pass, "it began to snow and the snow caked the ground. . . . The cold was intense." After several days of hard travel, Cortés and his men came down through the mountains and entered the Valley of Mexico, near the city of Chalco. The people of Chalco greeted them and gave them presents of gold and cloth. They also told Cortés about their harsh treatment by

"After the dying in Cholula, [the Spaniards] set off on
their way to Mexico. . . . Their iron lances and halberds
[battle-axes] seemed to sparkle, and their iron swords
were curved like a stream of water. Their cuirasses
[armor] and iron helmets seemed to make a clattering
sound. . . . Their dogs came in front, coming ahead of
them, . . . panting, with their spittle hanging down."
—Florentine Codex

the Mexica. Here was yet another native society that seemed
eager to escape the control of the Mexica empire.

Motecuzoma had hoped never to see the Spaniards
in Tenochtitlan. But once they were on his doorstep, he
welcomed them with the courtesy that the Mexica always
showed to important visitors. He sent his nephew Cacama,
the ruler of Texcoco, to meet Cortés and escort him into
Tenochtitlan. On November 8, 1519, Hernán Cortés and his
men entered the capital of the Mexica empire. Writing more
than forty years after that memorable day, the old soldier
Bernal Díaz described the scene:

> Gazing on such wonderful sights, we did not know
> what to say, or whether what appeared before us was
> real, for on one side, on the land, there were great
> cities, and in the lake ever so many more, . . . and in
> front of us stood the great City of Mexico, and we—
> we did not even number four hundred soldiers!

CHAPTER FIVE

THE CITY IN THE LAKE

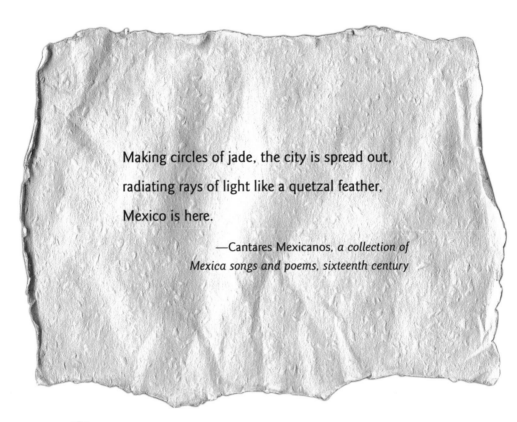

Making circles of jade, the city is spread out,

radiating rays of light like a quetzal feather,

Mexico is here.

—Cantares Mexicanos, *a collection of
Mexica songs and poems, sixteenth century*

Cortés and his men entered Tenochtitlan from the south,
crossing the causeway that led from the town of Iztapalapa.
At the end of the causeway, Motecuzoma and his escorts were
waiting to receive them. Díaz gives a vivid picture of the scene:

> The Great Montezuma was richly attired . . . and he
> was shod with sandals, and . . . the soles were of gold
> and the upper part adorned with precious stones. . . .

When Cortés was told that the Great Montezuma was approaching, . . . he dismounted from his horse, and when he was near Montezuma, they simultaneously paid great reverence to one another. Montezuma bade him welcome and our Cortés replied through Doña Marina wishing him very good health.

Gifts were exchanged, and the emperor made a formal speech. When speaking at public ceremonies, the Mexica always used high-flown language filled with courteous phrases. Motecuzoma addressed Cortés in this manner:

Our lord, you are weary. The journey has tired you, but now you have arrived. . . . You have come to your city, Mexico. You have come here to sit on your throne, to sit under its canopy. . . . Rest now, and take possession of your royal houses. Welcome to your land, my lords.

This version of Motecuzoma's speech came from the Mexica people whom Sahagún interviewed for his book. Cortés's second letter to King Charles includes another version, in very different language but with the same underlying message. The emperor seemed to be welcoming Cortés as the rightful ruler of Tenochtitlan. Some modern historians think that Motecuzoma's words reflect the exaggerated courtesy that the Mexica showed all visitors and were not meant literally. Others wonder whether the accounts of the emperor's speech may have been rewritten in the light of later events.

This image shows Cortés and his translator Malinche meeting with Motecuzoma in Tenochtitlan. It comes from the Lienzo *(Spanish for "canvas")* de Tlaxcala, *a pictorial work produced in the city of Tlaxcala in the 1500s. The eighty drawings in the work depict the conquest of Mexico from the Tlaxcalan point of view.*

Whether or not Motecuzoma truly intended to hand Tenochtitlan over to the Spaniards, Cortés was ready to seize the opportunity. He thanked the emperor for his courtesy and followed him into the city. Most of the Tlaxcalans who had accompanied the expedition stayed outside.

STRANGE AND MARVELOUS THINGS

Motecuzoma provided housing for his visitors in the palace of his father, who had ruled the Mexica in the late 1400s. This grand building, "coated with shining cement and swept and garlanded," was located on Tenochtitlan's main plaza.

In his letter to the king, Cortés reported, "In order to

give an account . . . of the magnificence, the strange and marvelous things of this great city, . . . I would need much time and many expert narrators." Nevertheless, he went on to describe the beautiful palaces and the impressive temples, "which are of remarkable size . . . and decorated with many designs and sculptures."

In the company of Cortés and other members of the expedition, Bernal Díaz visited the great marketplace in Tlatelolco. "We were astounded at the number of people and the quantity of merchandise . . . , and at the good order and control that was maintained." All kinds of food products were available: "beans and sage and other vegetables and herbs,"; "fowls [probably turkeys], rabbits, hares, deer, mallards, young dogs."; "and other dainties like nut paste."

Díaz was overwhelmed by the variety. "Why do I waste so many words in recounting all they sell in that great market?—for I shall never finish if I tell it all in detail."

When Díaz and the other Spaniards saw Tenochtitlan's many temples, they were stunned and horrified. Motecuzoma himself gave Cortés and his men permission to visit the temple of Huitzilopochtli at the top of the steep pyramid on the city's main square. Díaz described the image of the war god with its "broad face and monstrous and terrible eyes" and its body "girdled by great snakes made of gold and precious stones." The interior walls of the temple "were so splashed and encrusted with blood that they were black, the floor was the same and the whole place stank vilely." There were also "braziers [small grills] with incense which they call copal, and in them they were burning the hearts of three Indians whom they had sacrificed that day."

After visiting the temple, Cortés told Motecuzoma that "these idols of yours are not gods, but evil things that are called devils." Díaz reported that the emperor defended the Mexica gods, saying, "We consider them to be very good for they give us health and rains and good seed times . . . and as many victories as we desire, and we are obliged to worship them and make sacrifices, and I pray you not to say another word to their dishonour." After hearing these words, Cortés asked pardon for his remarks. The time for a confrontation over religion had not yet arrived.

CORTÉS TAKES COMMAND

During his first few days in Tenochtitlan, Cortés met frequently with Motecuzoma. Speaking through the interpreters Malinche and Aguilar, the two men conversed politely and calmly. According to Díaz, the emperor told the Spaniards that "he was greatly rejoiced to have in his house and his kingdom such valiant gentlemen as were Cortés and all of us." Cortés thanked the emperor for his courtesy and told him about King Charles, "who held beneath his sway many and great princes." He also spoke about Christianity and "the one only true God" and promised that the king would send holy men to instruct the Mexica in this new faith.

The conversation may have been polite, but the situation was tense. Motecuzoma was still uncertain about the identity of his honored guests. Perhaps the Spaniards were those whom his ancestors had said "would come from where the sun rose to rule over these lands." Cortés also had reason to be uneasy. He and his men were surrounded by thousands of

Mexica who could overwhelm them at any time.

The tension boiled over about five days after the Spaniards' arrival in the city. Cortés received word that a Mexica army had attacked his Totonac allies near Vera Cruz. Several of the Spanish soldiers sent to aid the Totonacs were killed. With this act of rebellion as an excuse, Cortés took Motecuzoma hostage.

Everything was done with the greatest courtesy. Cortés persuaded the emperor that, until the incident with the Totonacs was resolved, it would be better if he left his palace and came to stay in the house where Cortés was living. Amazingly, the emperor agreed to go with Cortés. The all-powerful ruler of the Mexica had become a prisoner in his own city.

How could this have happened? Historians have argued about the subject for decades. Some think that Motecuzoma's weakness and indecision allowed Cortés to seize control. Ever since the Spaniards had entered his country, the emperor had not resisted them. He had even allowed the strangers to come into his capital city. His imprisonment was just one more step in a process that had started months before.

Other scholars think that there might have been political reasons for Motecuzoma's behavior. Some of the emperor's advisers had urged him to keep the Spaniards out of Tenochtitlan. These men might have been plotting to overthrow Motecuzoma and seize power. Perhaps by cooperating with the Spaniards, the emperor thought he would be able to keep his throne.

We have no way of knowing what was in the mind of Motecuzoma at this time. The outcome was clear, however. Although the emperor ruled Tenochtitlan in name, Hernán Cortés had become the power behind the Mexica throne.

TROUBLE ON ALL SIDES

With Motecuzoma as his prisoner, Cortés assumed that he
could take complete control of Tenochtitlan. The nobles of
the city were angered by the emperor's surrender, but they
were not willing to challenge his authority and fight Cortés.
Leaders in other nearby Mexica cities, however, were ready to
resist the Spaniards. Cacama, the king of Texcoco, along with
several other rulers, made plans to attack the Spanish invaders.
Motecuzoma heard about the plot and reported it to Cortés.

At Cortés's urging, the emperor sent six of his loyal
nobles to Texcoco with orders to capture Cacama and
bring him to Tenochtitlan. Cacama was imprisoned, and
Motecuzoma appointed one of his own sons to rule Texcoco
in his place. The other leaders of the rebellion were also
captured. The attack against the Spaniards had been averted,
but the resentment of the Mexica nobles continued to grow.

At this dangerous point, Cortés had to deal with another
crisis. The military force sent by Governor Velásquez in
Cuba had finally arrived on the Gulf Coast. Under the
command of Pánfilo de Narváez, more than one thousand
well-armed soldiers aboard nineteen ships landed near San
Juan de Ulua in April 1520. Narváez had orders to capture
Cortés and bring him back to Cuba.

Hearing this news, Cortés left Tenochtitlan and marched
to the coast, taking with him a small force of only 266 men.
The rest of the Spanish soldiers stayed in the city, under the
command of Pedro de Alvarado. Despite being outnumbered,
Cortés's small army was able to defeat Narváez's forces by
launching a surprise attack at night. Narváez was taken
prisoner, and most of his men joined Cortés. They had little

choice since Cortés had ordered Narváez's ships to be disabled, just as he had done earlier with the ships of his own expedition.

By defeating Narváez, Cortés had not only eliminated the threat from Governor Velásquez, but he had also strengthened his own forces. With more men, weapons, and horses, he could return to Tenochtitlan and continue his campaign against the Mexica.

Pedro de Alvarado

DISASTER IN TENOCHTITLAN

During the time that Cortés was dealing with Narváez, the situation in Tenochtitlan had taken a turn for the worse. Pedro de Alvarado was responsible for the disaster. He had ordered Spanish soldiers to attack a group of Mexica nobles who were gathered to celebrate the festival of Toxcatl. Many were killed or wounded, and the people of Tenochtitlan were outraged at this attack on unarmed men.

Why or how this happened is another historical puzzle. According to Bernal Díaz, Alvarado claimed he had heard that "as soon as they [the nobles] had finished the festival and dances and the sacrifices . . . , they would at once come and make an attack." He had attacked first to prevent this.

Other versions of the event are different. In his biography of Cortés, López de Gómara said that Alvarado and his men had gone to watch the Mexica festival and "the strange and marvelous dance." Seeing the gold and jewels worn by the dancers, the Spaniards had "without any Christian respect slew and murdered them all and took from them all their treasure."

The Mexica gave their own account of the slaughter, recorded in the *Florentine Codex.* The festival of Toxcatl was held every year in honor of Huitzilopochtli. Both Cortés and Alvarado had given permission for the festival to take place, and the participants "had sworn to dance and sing with all their hearts, so that the Spaniards would marvel at the beauty of the ritual." In the courtyard in front of the temple, the warriors performed the Dance of the Serpent. "The great captains, the bravest warriors, danced at the head of the files to guide the others."

At the moment "when the dance was loveliest and when song was linked to song," the Spaniards attacked. "They ran in among the dancers, forcing their way to the place where the drums were played. They attacked the man who was drumming and cut off his arms. Then they cut off his head, and it rolled across the floor. . . . They attacked all the celebrants, stabbing them, spearing them, striking them with their swords. . . . The blood of the warriors flowed like water and gathered into pools."

The Mexica account, like López de Gómara's, seems to suggest that the attack was unprovoked. Certainly that was how it seemed to the people of Tenochtitlan. When the news spread, "a great cry went up: 'Mexicanos, come running! Bring your spears and shields! The strangers have murdered our warriors.'" Mexica forces attacked Alvarado and his men.

THE FESTIVAL OF TOXCATL

The festival of Huitzilopochtli, held during the month of Toxcatl, was one of the most important of the Mexica festivals. Sahagún said, "It was like our Easter and fell at almost the same time."

In preparation for the celebration, women made a statue of the war god out of the seeds of the amaranth plant. They ground the seeds into a paste and shaped the figure *(at right, top)* over a framework of sticks, giving it "such a human appearance that it seemed the body of a living man." The statue was dressed in "a magic headdress of humming-bird feathers" and a vest "painted with dismembered human parts: skulls, ears, hearts, . . . hands and feet." Before this fearsome image, participants in the festival performed their "strange and marvelous dance."

A set of illustrations from the Florentine Codex *depicts the festival of Toxcatl, which ends with a sacrifice to Huitzilopochtli.*

At least seven Spaniards were killed, and the rest took refuge in the palace where Motecuzoma was being held. Alvarado and his men used artillery to fight off the continuing Mexica attack, but the Spaniards could not escape from the palace.

When Cortés heard what had happened in Tenochtitlan, he left the coast and headed back to the city, with an army of about fifteen hundred Spaniards and two thousand Tlaxcalans. On June 24, 1520, they entered the Mexica capital, meeting no resistance. The streets of the city were silent and deserted.

BESIEGED IN THE CITY

Cortés rejoined his comrades in the palace, hoping to regain control. He confronted Alvarado and told him that his attack on the nobles at the festival "was very ill done and a great mistake." His rash actions had aroused the anger of the Mexica and drove them to turn on the Spaniards.

For twenty-three days, Cortés and his men were besieged in their palace by Mexica soldiers armed with javelins and bows. Although the Spaniards were able to beat back the attacks with firearms, they could not escape. When parties of Spanish soldiers ventured out, they were bombarded by rocks thrown from the rooftops of buildings and were forced to retreat. Supplies were running low. As the situation became more desperate, Cortés tried to negotiate a peace settlement so that his forces could withdraw from the city. He ordered Motecuzoma, still a prisoner in the palace, to address the people of Tenochtitlan and ask them to stop the violence.

The emperor was taken to the roof of the palace, where

"he began to speak to his people, with very affectionate expressions telling them to desist from the war, and that we [the Spaniards] would leave Mexico." Díaz reported Motecuzoma's words and then described what happened next. The emperor was struck "by a shower of stones and darts" and received a mortal wound. "His own people killed him with blows from three stones."

Some Mexica accounts claim that Spaniards killed Motecuzoma, "stabbing him in the abdomen with their swords." It is impossible to know which account is true, but at this point, the emperor was of little use to Cortés as a hostage. His authority had been weakened, and the Mexica were refusing to obey him. It might have seemed simpler to get rid of him.

Surrounded by Spanish soldiers, Moctecuzoma speaks to the Mexica people from the roof of a palace. This painting is part of the Conquest of Mexico series based on Solís's history.

During the short mourning period after Motecuzoma's death, the attacks on the Spaniards ceased. The Mexica nobles chose a new ruler, Cuitlahuac, a brother of Motecuzoma who had consistently opposed Cortés. Under his leadership, the Mexica resumed their assaults on the Spanish stronghold. Díaz wrote: "Although we fought like brave men we could not drive [the Mexica] back. . . . The powder was giving out, and the same was happening with the food and water. . . . We were staring death in the face." If Cortés and his men did not escape from Tenochtitlan, they would surely be killed.

LA NOCHE TRISTE

The only way out of the city in the lake was over one of the causeways that led to the shore. Cortés chose the western causeway leading to the city of Tlacopan because it seemed to be the shortest. He decided to make his escape by night, hoping to avoid detection by the Mexica.

In preparation for their flight, the Spaniards packed the gold, silver, and jewels they had collected. Even though they were running for their lives, they could not leave their loot behind. The king's share of the treasure was loaded onto horses or put in packs to be carried by Tlaxcalan porters. The burdens were heavy because most of the gold jewelry and ornaments had been melted down into bars.

After this was done, "much gold still remained in the Hall piled up in heaps." Cortés told his men to take what they wanted. Bernal Díaz took only a few chalchihuites, the green stones that were so precious to the Mexica. He declared: "I had no other desire but the desire to save my life."

It was raining when the Spaniards crept out of their fortified palace around midnight on June 30, 1520. Leading the retreat was a group of soldiers guarding several important "companions" of the Spaniards—Doña Marina (Malinche), Cortés's interpreter and mistress, and Doña Luisa, Pedro de Alvarado's mistress—along with the expedition's three priests. Cortés and the bulk of the army followed, and Alvarado brought up the rear. Also in the group were Mexica hostages that the Spaniards had captured and still held, among them a son and two daughters of Motecuzoma.

Because the Mexica had removed the causeway bridges, the Spaniards carried with them a portable wooden bridge to cross the open spaces. The portable bridge did its job, and the expedition crossed safely over three of the gaps in the causeway. The main body of Spaniards had almost reached the outskirts of the city when they were discovered. According to the *Florentine Codex*, a woman coming to draw water from a canal saw them and raised the alarm.

The Mexica warriors rushed to their canoes "and paddled hard, hitting one another's boats as they went. . . . The war boats came upon them from both directions; the war boats of the Tenocha [the people of Tenochtitlan] and the war boats of the Tlatelolca [the people of the Tlatelolco district]." From the canoes, Mexica warriors threw barbed darts at the men trapped on the causeway. The Spaniards fought back "with iron bolts [arrows] and guns," and there were many deaths on both sides.

At the head of the Spanish line, Cortés and the men with him were able to fight off the Mexica forces and reach the shore of the lake, along with Doña Marina and Doña

Luisa. Leaving the women there, Cortés returned to help those still struggling on the causeway.

By this time, the Mexica had destroyed the portable bridge, and the Spaniards could not cross the openings in the causeway. Many were forced into the water, along with all their weapons, baggage, and the heavy gold bars they were carrying. At the gap over the Toltec canal, "it was as though they had fallen off a precipice," reported the *Florentine Codex*. "They all fell and dropped in, the Tlaxcalans . . . and the Spaniards, along with the horses and some women. The canal was completely full of them, full to the very top. And those who came last just passed and crossed over on people, on bodies."

Completely cut off, those at the end of the Spanish line fled back to the palace on Tenochtitlan's main square. They held out for a few days, but were eventually captured by the Mexica and offered as sacrifices to the gods. Many of these were men who had come to Mexico with Narváez.

Those Spaniards who had escaped struggled to reach the city of Tlacopan, pursued by bands of Mexica warriors. Cortés and many of his captains, including Alvarado, made it to safety. But there had been heavy losses of both men and equipment. According to modern estimates, at least six hundred Spaniards and about two thousand Tlaxcalans had been killed. Many of the expedition's horses and all the cannon were lost. All the gold disappeared, probably sunk to the bottom of the lake. The royal captives and the Mexica nobles who had sided with Cortés died during the escape.

Those Spaniards who survived the flight from Tenochtitlan on June 30, 1520, remembered the event as La

Noche Triste, "the Sad Night." On this night, the Mexica had finally turned on their unwanted visitors and attacked them with courage and fierceness. Despite the advantage of their artillery and steel weapons, the Spaniards had been forced to flee for their lives. Hernán Cortés' dream of conquering the Mexica seemed at an end, but he was not ready to give up yet.

"It was pitiable to see our wounds being dressed and bound up with cotton cloth. . . . However even more to be wept over was the loss of the gentlemen and brave soldiers who were missing, namely, Juan Velásquez de Leon, Francisco de Sauzedo, . . . and many others of us followers of Cortés. . . . Let us go on to say how there were left dead at the bridges the sons and daughters of Montezuma as well as the [other] prisoners we were bringing with us, also Cacamatzin the Lord of Texcoco and other kings of provinces."
—*Bernal Díaz del Castillo, describing La Noche Triste*

CHAPTER SIX

RETURN TO THE CITY

I am glad to find you armed and eager to return to Mexico
to avenge the deaths of our comrades and recover that
great city. This, I trust in God, we shall soon do . . . , for
Spaniards dare face the greatest peril, consider fighting
their glory, and have the habit of winning.

—*Cortés's address to his army, December 1520*

After Cortés and his men made their escape from
Tenochtitlan, Mexica warriors followed them and continued
the attack. The two sides fought almost continuously as the
Spanish forces moved around the lake toward the territory
of the Tlaxcalans. Eventually, the Mexica gave up the
pursuit. Problems at home seemed more pressing than any
threat from the defeated Spaniards. Buildings, streets, and
causeways destroyed in the battle had to be reconstructed.

Even more important, Tenochtitlan's government had been seriously weakened by the death of Motecuzoma and the battle with the Spaniards. Cities such as Texcoco and Chalco might not continue to support Tenochtitlan if it could not enforce their loyalty.

In the days following his escape from the Mexica capital, Cortés had his own problems. Almost all his men had been wounded during the retreat, and they needed time to recover. Some were talking openly about giving up the fight against the Mexica and returning to Cuba.

Cortés was also concerned about his native allies. Tlaxcala and the other allied cities had been impressed by the weapons and the military skill of the Spaniards. Would they continue their support after witnessing their new friends' humiliating defeat at the hands of the Mexica?

Luckily for Cortés, Tlaxcala, his major ally, decided to stay on the Spanish side. When the expedition reached Tlaxcalan territory in July 1520, the city leaders came out to meet Cortés and pledged their support, for a price. The Tlaxcalans wanted to divide the spoils of the Mexica empire equally with the Spaniards. Cortés accepted their terms. He knew that without the aid of the Tlaxcalan armies, he had no chance of defeating the Mexica.

A DEADLY ENEMY

During the chaotic period following the Spanish escape from Tenochtitlan, another deadly force made its appearance on the scene. A smallpox epidemic devastated central Mexico, killing native people on both sides of the conflict.

This European disease had already attacked the inhabitants of Hispaniola and Cuba, reducing the populations there by as much as 90 percent. It reached Mexico in April 1520, probably brought by one of the men in the Narváez expedition. Smallpox spread quickly because native people had no immunity to it. It devastated the Maya of the Yucatán and the Totonacs who lived near the coast.

By the middle of October in 1520, the disease had reached the Valley of Mexico. In Tenochtitlan the smallpox epidemic lasted from mid-October until early December 1520. Among the thousands who died was Motecuzoma's

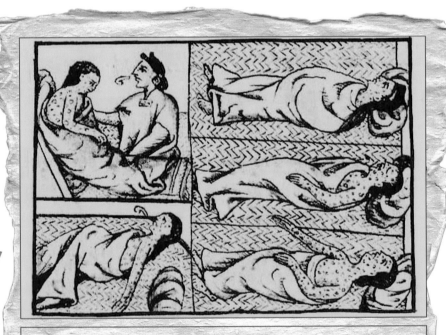

An illustration from the Florentine Codex showing victims of smallpox. "We were covered with agonizing sores from head to foot," the Mexica said. "The sick were so utterly helpless that they could only lie on their beds like corpses."

successor, Cuitlahuac. Other cities in the Valley of Mexico such as Chalco and Tlacopan also lost their rulers to the disease. Maxixcatzin, one of the leaders of Tlaxcala and a firm supporter of Cortés, was also a victim. To the amazement of their allies, the Spaniards did not seem to get the disease. Because smallpox was a common childhood illness in Europe, many Spaniards had become resistant to it.

The devastation caused by smallpox only added to the confusion and political turmoil in the Mexica empire. Populations in some areas were reduced by as much as 40 percent. New leaders with little experience or support replaced the old rulers who had died in the epidemic.

In Tenochtitlan, Cuauhtemoc, a young relative of Cuitlahuac (and of Motecuzoma) was chosen as the supreme ruler of the Mexica. Only in his mid-twenties, Cuauhtemoc had already proven himself in battle. He had been a leader in the Tlatelolco district of Tenochtitlan, and he was popular among the surviving nobles of the city.

PREPARATIONS FOR BATTLE

Even before the end of the smallpox epidemic, Cortés was preparing to renew his attack on the Mexica. As a part of his plan, Cortés decided that he needed a naval force. During the retreat from Tenochtitlan, Mexica control of the lake had been a deciding factor in the defeat of the Spaniards, and Cortés was determined that it would not happen again. He ordered Martín López, a shipbuilder who was a member of his expedition, to construct thirteen brigantines that the Spaniards could take into battle.

"Martín López made such speed in the cutting the wood with the great assistance rendered him by the Indians, that he had the whole of it cut within a few days, and each beam marked for the position for which it was intended to occupy."

—Bernal Díaz del Castillo, late 1500s

The work would be done at Tlaxcala, a safe territory but far from the shores of Lake Texcoco. Timber was cut in the nearby forests. Other needed supplies came from the Spanish ships that had been grounded in Vera Cruz. Bernal Díaz said that Cortés "sent for much of the iron and the bolts of the ships which we had destroyed, and for anchors, sails and rigging and for cables and . . . all the other material for building ships."

With the help of the Tlaxcalans, López and his assistants constructed the brigantines, which were equipped with both oars and sails. The finished ships would be taken apart and the pieces would be carried across the mountains to the shores of the great lake.

With his navy under construction, Cortés gathered other supplies. He found a ready source in some Spanish ships that had recently landed at Vera Cruz. Velásquez had sent several expeditions to find out what had happened to Pánfilo de Narváez, who was supposed to have captured Cortés. Other ships had brought Spaniards from Cuba and Hispaniola. They had heard about Cortés's discoveries in Mexico and wanted to join in the plunder. One vessel had even come from Spain, sent by Cortés's father and friends back home. It was "laden with a great variety of merchandise, muskets, powder, crossbows and crossbow cords and three horses and other arms."

Cortés wasted no time in taking advantage of this new source of supplies. Using a combination of threats and promises, he convinced most of the ships' crews to join him, adding about two hundred men to his army.

With additional men and a new supply of weapons, Cortés was ready to begin his campaign against the Mexica. Central to his plan was cutting off Tenochtitlan from the rest of the empire. To do this, the Spaniards attacked Tepeyacac and other cities on the eastern side of the lake that sent tribute to the Mexica capital. Overwhelmed by Spanish cavalry and firepower, they pledged to support Cortés.

Although battles continued between Spanish and Mexica forces east of the lake, the leaders in Tenochtitlan did not send out large armies to defend the tributary cities. One reason may have been lack of manpower. Because the Spanish attacks took place during the rainy season, most of the men who made up the Mexica army were working in the fields. Mexica wars usually took place during the dry season from October to June, when ordinary soldiers were not busy farming.

Rather than meet the Spaniards in open combat, Cuauhtemoc and his advisers may have decided to make the enemy come to Tenochtitlan. If the Mexica could lure the Spaniards into the city, they could fight them on the causeways, where horses and cavalry charges were of little use. This approach had worked during the earlier battle, and it could work again.

This statue of Cuauhtemoc stands on the Avenida de la Reforma, one of the main streets in modern Mexico City.

On December 28, 1520, Cortés assembled his forces in the main square at Tlaxcala. According to López de Gómara, Cortés addressed his men, saying "I am glad to find you armed and eager to return to Mexico to avenge the deaths of our comrades and recover that great city." But revenge was not the only reason for defeating the Mexica. "Let us go, then, and serve God, honor our nation, magnify our King, and enrich ourselves, for the conquest of Mexico is all these things."

After this inspiring speech, the Spanish forces and their ten thousand Tlaxclan allies set off in the direction of Texcoco, a large and prosperous community located east of the great lake. Texcoco was the most important city in the Mexica empire after Tenochtitlan. One of the members of the Triple Alliance, it had played a key role in the defeat of the Tepanecs in 1428.

When Cortés entered Texcoco, he found the streets silent and deserted. Many of the city's inhabitants, including those nobles who supported the Mexica, had fled to Tenochtitlan. With the bloodless defeat of Texcoco, a major piece in Cortés's plan fell into place. He had a base of operations near the lake and a ready source of food and other supplies. The rulers of Texcoco would support the Spaniards in the coming conflict, not their old ally Tenochtitlan.

FINAL OBSTACLES

Texcoco was an important conquest, but other cities near the lake were still under Mexica control. Chalco, at the far southern end, was one of them. Cortés thought that he could win the leaders of Chalco to his side, but first he had to defeat the Mexica forces guarding the city. Taking half of his army, he marched from Texcoco to Ixtapalapan, where the Mexica troops were stationed.

In the ensuing battle, the Spaniards captured Ixtapalapan and occupied the city, which was located on a low-lying peninsula in the lake. Bernal Díaz said that he and the other soldiers had settled into their quarters, "well contented with the spoils we had taken and still more with the victory we had gained." But their good mood did not last. "When we least expected it . . . a flood of water rushed through the whole town. . . . The enemy had burst open the canals . . . and torn down the causeway, so that the water rose up all of a sudden." Some of the Spanish soldiers drowned, while the rest escaped to higher ground. Pursued by Mexica warriors, they finally reached safety in Texcoco.

This was the first major battle that the Spaniards had fought since they entered the Valley of Mexico, and it had not been a great success. Again, some of Cortés's men were concerned about their situation. They wanted to end the fighting and leave Mexico for good. With Spanish ships coming regularly to Vera Cruz, they knew that they could find a way back to Cuba.

The leader of the rebellious group was Antonio de Villafaña, "a great friend of the Governor of Cuba [Velásquez]," according to Díaz. The rebels made plans to assassinate Cortés, but the plot was discovered. Villafaña was quickly put on trial for treason, found guilty, and hanged.

With his men under control, Cortés continued his efforts to isolate Tenochtitlan. He repeatedly fought the Mexica at Chalco and eventually defeated them. Freed from Mexica control, Chalco joined the Spanish side. Other cities in the region followed its example. The Mexica empire, which had been held together only by military might, seemed to be crumbling.

Cuauhtemoc and his advisers were doing all they could to prevent this from happening. In addition to sending small military forces to attack the Spaniards, the leaders of Tenochtitlan tried to convince the rulers of other cities in the empire to continue their support. They sent lavish presents and offered to drop the demand for tribute.

These tactics were generally unsuccessful. The Mexica had long been the supreme power in central Mexico, and other cities had no choice but to bow to their rule. Cortés and the Spaniards seemed to offer a means to escape Mexica control. Texcoco, Chalco, and other cities did not join Cortés out of any loyalty to the Spanish leader and his cause. Instead, they believed that, in siding with the Spaniards, they would improve their own political and economic situations.

If the rulers of these cities could have seen the future, they would have realized that a Spanish victory would not only end Mexica rule but also bring about other drastic changes. Their world would be turned upside down.

CHAPTER SEVEN
THE FINAL BATTLE

Proud of itself

is the city of Mexico-Tenochtitlan.

Here no one fears to die in war. . . .

Have this in mind, oh princes,

Do not forget it.

Who could conquer Tenochtitlan?

Who could shake the foundations of heaven?

> —Cantares Mexicanos, *a collection of*
> *Mexica songs and poems, sixteenth century*

In early 1521, Hernán Cortés began his assault on Tenochtitlan, the heart of the Mexica empire. As a first step, he led his forces in an attack on the city of Tlacopan, located at the end of the western causeway. The Spaniards were able to capture the city, but when they moved out on the causeway leading to Tenochtitlan, they were driven back by large numbers of Mexica warriors. Other Mexica forces attacked from canoes on both sides of the causeway, just as had happened during the Spanish flight from the city in July 1520.

The Spaniards occupied Tlacopan for several days, but on February 18, they retreated to Texcoco. Cortés's troops had more success with other strongholds such as Cuauhnahuac (modern Cuernavaca), located in a valley south of the lake. When the Spaniards returned to the lakeshore on April 16, however, they met another defeat at Xochimilco.

The Mexica were still in control of the lake, but that was soon to change. The brigantines built in Tlaxcala were ready to be put into action. They had been brought to Texcoco by "eight thousand men [Tlaxcalans] carrying on their backs all the timbers and boards." The shipbuilder Martín López and his helpers worked with "the greatest dispatch" to put the brigantines together.

Because Texcoco was located several miles from the lakeshore, a canal had to be dug to launch the ships. López de Gómara reported that forty thousand men from Texcoco worked on the canal, which was more than 12 feet (3.7 meters) wide and 12 feet deep. By the end of April 1521, the canal was finished. The ships "were already built and had their rigging, sails, and oars in place." All was ready for the final campaign.

BATTLE PLANS

In the great plaza of Texcoco, Cortés reviewed his forces. The Spanish army had increased in size since 1520 with the addition of men who had come from Cuba and Hispaniola to join Cortés. According to Díaz, "There were present eighty-four horsemen, six-hundred-and-fifty soldiers with swords and shields and many with lances, and one-hundred-and-ninety-four crossbowmen and musketeers." In addition to the muskets, the army had some small cannons that could be mounted on the brigantines. The shot and gunpowder for the weapons had come from the Spanish ships at Vera Cruz.

The brigantines would play a major role in the coming battle, and Cortés selected their crews himself. "For each launch, [there were] twelve crossbowmen and musketeers; in addition . . . , there were also set apart another twelve men . . . as rowers." Each ship also had an artilleryman and, of course, a captain.

Cortés himself would lead the fleet of brigantines and act as commander in chief of the army. The land forces were divided into three separate groups. Pedro de Alvarado, well known by Spaniards and natives for his reckless courage, would lead one division. He would take up a position at Tlacopan. A second division commanded by Cristóbal de Olid would establish a base at Coyohuacan. This city was located at the end of the southwestern causeway, the longest

SPANISH WEAPONS

The Spanish arsenal of weapons included steel-bladed swords and lances, which were used by foot soldiers and cavalry. The crossbow was another formidable weapon. This heavy bow fired wooden arrows with metal heads over a distance of 1,000 feet (305 m). Spanish artillery included falconets, smaller cannons that could be attached to the rail of a ship. The main firearm the troops carried was the harquebus, an early kind of musket. A harquebus fired a lead ball and had to be reloaded after each shot. In battle Spanish soldiers usually wore steel helmets and body armor and carried metal shields.

of those leading into Tenochtitlan. The leader of the third army was Gonzalo de Sandoval. He would take a stand near Ixtapalapan, at the southern end of the lake.

Each division of the Spanish army included at least twenty thousand native warriors from Tlaxcala, Chalco, Texcoco, and other allies. Spaniards made up only about one percent of the forces that would sweep down on Tenochtitlan. In the coming battle, the people of Mexico would fight one another for supremacy, but the Spaniards would be the winners.

FIRST ENCOUNTERS

On May 22, 1521, the Spanish and allied armies marched out of Texcoco with flags and feathered banners waving. Cortés stayed behind to oversee the launching of the brigantines. The forces of Alvarado and Olid went to Tlacopan and then on to the city of Chapultepec, west of the lake.

Chapultepec was a strategic spot. The city supplied fresh springwater to Tenochtitlan through an aqueduct built in 1499. (Most of the lake water was too salty to drink.) The Spaniards attacked the Mexica forces defending Chapultepec and cut both channels of the aqueduct. "From this time onwards," said Bernal Díaz, "[the water] never flowed into Mexico [Tenochtitlan] so long as the war lasted."

After destroying the aqueduct, the armies of Olid and Alvarado returned to Tlacopan and again attempted to cross the causeway leading into Tenochtitlan. Fighting with Alvarado's army, Bernal Díaz was in the midst of the action. "When we reached the causeway, there were so many canoes on the lake full of warriors and the causeways were so crowded with them, that we were astonished at it; and they shot so many arrows and javelins and stones from slings that at the first encounter they wounded over thirty soldiers."

The Spaniards fired their cannons and muskets at the Mexica on the causeway and killed many in the front line, but hundreds of other warriors were ready to take their place. The Mexica soldiers soon developed tactics to deal with the Spanish weapons. Since the shots from the artillary flew in a straight line, "they ran to the right or left or in zigzags, not in front of the guns," reported the *Florentine Codex*. "If . . . they could not escape by running, they threw themselves to the ground and lay flat until the shot had passed over them."

The Spanish and Mexica forces fought on the Tlacopan causeway for several days, often engaging in hand-to-hand combat. Finally, under attack from both land and water,

MEXICA WEAPONS

The Mexica fought with weapons not of steel but of wood and stone. Their swords, lances, and clubs were made of wood with blades of sharp obsidian embedded in them. Mexica warriors were also armed with short spears and darts, which they threw with the aid of the atlatl, or throwing stick. Mexica soldiers also used the slingshot and the bow and arrow. In battle the elite Mexica warriors were protected by armor made of padded cotton, which they wore under garments of woven feathers or animal skins. Army commanders had tall wicker structures decorated with feathers strapped to their backs. These made it easy for soldiers to find their leaders in the thick of battle.

the Spaniards withdrew. Alvarado made camp at the city of Tlacopan, while Olid led his army south to Coyohuacan. Sandoval's army had reached Ixtapalapan and had established a base there. The next stage in the battle would be up to Cortés.

THE BRIGANTINES ARRIVE

On May 30, 1521, Cortés launched the thirteen brigantines into Lake Texcoco. The Spanish ships were met by a fleet of five hundred Mexica canoes sent out from Tenochtitlan. In the ensuing battle, the brigantines easily outmaneuvered the native vessels, ramming them and tipping them over. Some of the canoes escaped into canals that were too narrow for the Spanish ships, but the brigantines had proved their worth.

After this first naval victory, the Spanish fleet sailed toward Coyohuacan, where Olid's army was fighting the Mexica. Cortés ordered his native allies to make a break in the Coyohuacan causeway so that the brigantines could sail through. With ships on both sides of the causeway, the Spaniards were able to repel the Mexica canoes attacking Olid's forces.

Once Coyohuacan was secured, the brigantines headed off to aid Sandoval, who was coming from Ixtapalapan to join Olid's army. Again taking up positions on both sides of the causeways, the ships fought off attacks on Sandoval and his men, allowing them to reach Coyohuacan on May 31, 1521.

The brigantines were proving very useful to the Spanish forces. They could go anywhere on the lake, delivering weapons and supplies where they were needed. The cannons mounted on the brigantines could be brought close to the action and fired at Mexica warriors on the causeways or in canoes.

Faced with this new kind of warfare, the Mexica came up with methods to deter the ships. In areas of shallow water, they embedded sharp stakes in the lake floor that could penetrate the brigantines' hulls. To lure the Spanish ships into these traps, they sent out a few canoes as decoys. When the brigantines pursued the decoys, the Mexica launched a fleet of canoes to drive the Spanish ships into the stakes.

Despite such efforts, the Mexica could not overcome the brigantines and the firearms that they carried. But they could continue to fight with the weapons of their ancestors—the spears, darts, arrows, and obsidian-bladed axes that had won so many battles in the past.

BATTLE ON THE CAUSEWAYS

The brigantines gave the Spaniards control of the lake, but they were too small to transport troops or horses into battle. To capture Tenochtitlan, the Spanish forces would have to cross the causeways.

"Two of the brigantines, both with cannons mounted in their bows, attacked a flotilla of our shielded canoes. [The war canoes had wooden planks on their sides to reinforce them.] The cannons were fired into the thick of the flotilla. . . . Many of our warriors were killed outright; others drowned because they were too crippled by their wounds to swim away. The water was red with the blood of the dead and dying."

—Florentine Codex

In the Capture of Tenochtitlan *from the Conquest of Mexico series of paintings, Spanish and Mexica forces fight hard on the causeways. Brigantines battle canoes in the water.*

Fighting on the causeways was difficult and slow. With the help of the brigantines, the armies of Alvarado and Sandoval were able to gain ground during the day. At night, however, the Spaniards and their allies retreated to their camps on the shore. "Whenever we left a bridge or barricade unguarded after having captured it with much labour," Díaz wrote, "the enemy would retake and deepen it that same night, and construct stronger defences." When the Spaniards returned, they had to fight to recover the lost ground.

Finally, the Spanish armies began to make camp at wide spots or plazas on the causeways so that they could defend their positions. By using this defensive method, the Spanish forces were able to make better progress over the causeways leading to the city.

This scene from the Lienzo de Tlaxacla shows Spanish and Mexica forces fighting during the battle for Tenochtitlan. The canal is filled with Spanish soldiers and Mexica warriors in canoes.

By the beginning of June 1521, the defenders of Tenochtitlan were running short of food and water. The causeways were blocked, and the brigantines and allied canoes patrolled the lake, making it difficult to bring in supplies by water. Some food was stored in Tenochtitlan's warehouses, and a few wells provided drinking water. But this was not enough to feed a population of two hundred thousand people.

INTO THE HEART OF THE CITY

With the Mexica weakened by food shortages and constant fighting, Cortés decided to make a final drive into

Tenochtitlan. He would lead an army along the southern causeway into the city. Alvarado's forces would come from the west and Sandoval's from the north. If Cortés's plan worked, the Spaniards and their allies would meet at the great temple plaza in the heart of the city.

On June 10, the push began. According to López de Gómara, Cortés left "very early that morning with more than two hundred Spaniards and some eighty thousand friends [native allies]." He "ordered the brigantines to sail alongside the causeway and protect both his flanks."

The Mexica had removed bridges and made gaps in the causeway, but the Spaniards found a way to get across. At some spots, the brigantines were used to bridge the openings, and the army walked over their decks to reach the other side. Other gaps were filled with rubble from nearby buildings that had been destroyed. The Spaniards "threw in the stones from the shattered wall, the roof beams and adobe bricks from the nearest houses," Díaz wrote, "anything they could find, until the surface of the fill was level with the causeway."

Moving forward in this way, Cortés and his men reached the Eagle Gate, which marked the official entry into the city of Tenochtitlan. They set up their cannons at the gate and "wasted no time as they loaded and fired. . . . The smoke belched out in black clouds that darkened the sky, as if night was falling." The Mexica defenders retreated, and Cortés marched through the streets of the city to the great square where the temples to Tlaloc and Huitzilopochtli stood on their towering pyramid.

Cortés had reached his goal, but the Mexica rallied to defend this sacred ground. This is the account from the *Florentine Codex*:

The priests of Huitzilopochtli immediately began to beat their great ritual drums from the top of the pyramid. The deep throbbing of the drums resounded over the city, calling the warriors to defend the shrine of their god. . . . The great captains . . . who had been fighting from their canoes now returned and landed. . . .

The Spaniards, seeing that an attack was imminent, tightened their ranks and clenched the hilts of their swords. The next moment, all was noise and confusion. The [Mexica] charged into the plaza from every direction, and the air was black with arrows and gunsmoke. The battle was so furious that both sides had to pull back.

While Cortés and his army had been forced to retreat from Tenochtitlan, Alvarado and Sandoval had never even made it that far. But the Spaniards were determined to continue their drive into the heart of the city. On June 15, Cortés fought his way back up the southern causeway, tearing down and burning buildings as he went. (His native allies did most of the work.) They used the rubble to close gaps in the causeways and to fill in some of the shallow canals. This provided a roadway for the mounted soldiers. Destroying the buildings also eliminated places where Mexica warriors could conceal themselves. The Spanish forces had often been attacked by warriors who threw rocks from the rooftops of buildings along their route.

The assault of June 15 was successful, and Cortés again reached the temple square. Other attacks followed, and by the end of June, the Spaniards controlled almost half of Tenochtitlan. Alvarado and Sandoval had brought their armies into the city, and more native allies had joined the Spaniards, encouraged by their success. Cuauhtemoc and his people had fought a valiant fight, but the odds were against them. If the Mexica surrendered, they might be able to save their city from complete destruction.

LAST STAND AT TLATELOLCO

Instead of surrendering, Cuauhtemoc and his advisers made plans for further resistance. They would abandon Tenochtitlan and move their forces to Tlatelolco, the site of the great marketplace that had so impressed the Spaniards. Though Tlatelolco had become part of Tenochtitlan, it still had its own leaders and warriors. They would play a major role in the defense of the city.

As part of the new plan, Cuauhtemoc moved his headquarters to Tlatelolco, and the statue of Huitzilopochtli was brought from the Great Temple of Tenochtitlan. The Mexica army concentrated its forces there, preparing for a new Spanish attack.

It came on June 30, when Cortés, Alvarado, and Sandoval led a three-pronged attack aimed at Tlatelolco. Cortés's forces fought their way into the district but were driven back by a large Mexica army. When they reached a ditch that was supposed to have been filled with rubble, they found it open and filled instead with water. Forced back by the advancing Mexica warriors, some of Cortés's men fell into the ditch, where they drowned or were captured by other warriors in canoes.

Cortés himself was almost captured as he struggled to help his men. He described the incident in his letter to the

The Mexica prepare to defend the temple pyramid of Huitzilopochtli in Tlatelolco in this illustration from the Aubin Codex. Warriors stand guard while priests beat drums at the foot of the pyramid steps.

king: "As I was so intent on rescuing the drowning, I neither saw nor gave a thought to the harm I might receive. Certain Indians then came to seize me and would have carried me off." Cortés was rescued by one of his men. His chief bodyguard, Antonio de Quinones, insisted that he leave the battle. Cortés reluctantly agreed and retreated from Tlatelolco, along with other members of his army who had survived the battle.

The Mexica had won a great victory at Tlatelolco, and they had the Spanish captives to prove it. Over sixty Spaniards had been taken in the battle, as well as several horses. Some of the men were executed immediately. Their severed heads were flung down in front of Alvarado and Sandoval, who were still fighting

> "The woman of Tlatelolco joined in the fighting. They struck at the enemy and shot arrows at them; they tucked up their skirts and dressed in the regalia of war."
>
> —Florentine Codex

in the city. The other Spaniards would meet the fate of all Mexica captives—they would be sacrificed to the gods.

Bernal Díaz and others in Alvarado's company witnessed the sacrifices from their camp near Tlatelolco. They heard the sound of drums and horns and looked toward the temple pyramid at the Tlatelolco marketplace, where they saw their comrades being carried up the steps.

When [the Mexica] got them up to a small square in front of the oratory, where their accursed idols are held, we saw them place plumes on the heads of many of them and with things like fans in their hands, they forced them to dance before Huichilobos [Huitzilopochtli], and after they had danced they immediately placed them on their backs on some . . . narrow stones, . . . and with stone knives they sawed open their chests and drew out their palpitating hearts and offered them to the idols.

The *Florentine Codex* describes what happened after the ceremony. "As soon as the sacrifices were finished, [the Mexica] ranged the Spaniards' heads in rows on pikes. They also lined up their horses' heads . . . and arranged them all so that the faces were toward the sun."

This illustration from the Florentine Codex *shows the heads of the Spaniards sacrificed at Tlatelolco displayed along with the heads of dead Spanish horses.*

The capture and sacrifice of their comrades was a great shock to the Spaniards and a major setback in their plan to conquer the Mexica. Hearing of this horrifying defeat, many of the allied forces quietly left the battle. The cities around the lake that had backed Cortés began to withdraw their support. By early July 1521, the Spaniards seemed to be on the brink of defeat.

It was not long, however, before the tide turned again, as it had so often during this long and complicated war. Cortés received word that Cuauhnahuac, one of his allies not on the lake, was under attack by a neighboring city. He sent a small force to defend Cuauhnahuac, as well as another ally who asked for his help. These actions impressed the native leaders who had lost confidence in Cortés. Just as silently as they had left, the allied armies began to return to the battle.

Although the Mexica had defeated the Spaniards at Tlatelolco, they had not been able to drive them from the city. Thousands of Mexica warriors had been killed or wounded, and their forces were reduced in size. While the Mexica army was shrinking, Cortés's forces were getting larger. More men were coming from Spanish ships in Vera Cruz, bringing with them gunpowder, weapons, and other supplies.

Famine had also devastated the Mexica defenders. Like all the people of Tenochtitlan, they were suffering from a severe shortage of food and water. "There was no fresh water to drink," says the *Florentine Codex*, "only stagnant water and the brine of the lake, and many people died of dysentery. The only food was lizards, swallows, corncobs and the salt grasses of the lake. The people . . . chewed on deerhide and pieces of leather. . . . They ate the bitterest weeds and even dirt."

Despite their suffering, the Mexica struggled on, fighting the Spaniards on the streets and causeways. The Spanish forces continued their destruction of the city, reducing houses, palaces, and temples to rubble and burning what was left. Cortés told the king, "Although it distressed me, I determined to burn them, for it distressed the enemy very much more."

During July, Cortés sent messages to Cuauhtemoc, pleading with him to surrender. Although several meetings were arranged and terms presented, the Mexica ruler never came to negotiate. He and his advisers seemed to have made a decision—they would fight to the bitter end.

"OUR CITY IS LOST AND DEAD"

The end came at Tlatelolco, where the Mexica forces were making their last stand. Alvarado led the Spanish attack, and the fighting was fierce and hand to hand. The Spaniards reached the marketplace in Tlatelolco about August 1. According to the *Florentine Codex*, mounted soldiers "rode through it in a great circle, stabbing and killing many of our warriors and trampling everything under their horses' hooves."

Díaz, fighting with Alvarado, was among the Spaniards who climbed the pyramid in the central plaza to reach the temple of Huitzilopochtli. "We ran great risk of our lives, but nevertheless we ascended the steps which . . . were one hundred and fourteen in number. . . . We set the oratories on fire and burned the idols, and we planted our banners."

The Mexica watched in horror as the wooden temple of Huitzilopochtli went up in flames. "The flames and smoke leaped high into the air with a terrible roar," the *Florentine Codex* reported. "The people wept when they saw their temple on fire; they wept and cried out."

As the Spanish forces steadily gained ground, the Mexica brought out their final weapon. Cuauhtemoc chose an outstanding warrior named Opochtzin, who put on the war costume of the Quetzal-Owl. This splendid costume decorated with quetzal and owl feathers was a cherished treasure of the Mexica. "This regalia belonged to my father, the great warrior Ahuitzotl," Cuauhtemoc said. "Terrify our enemies with it. . . . Let them behold it and tremble."

Carrying a long arrow with an obsidian tip, "the most important part of the regalia," the Quetzal-Owl warrior entered the battle, accompanied by four other important warriors.

The quetzal feather seemed to open out, making him appear even greater and more terrifying. When our enemies saw him approach, they quaked as if they thought a mountain were about to fall on them. . . . The Quetzal-Owl climbed up onto a rooftop. When our enemies saw him, they came forward and prepared to attack him, but he succeeded in driving

them away. Then he came down from the rooftop
with his quetzal feathers and his gold ornaments.

After this, the Quetzal-Owl seems to have disappeared
into the thick of the battle. The *Florentine Codex* says that
he was not killed or captured but tells nothing about his later
actions. Spanish accounts of the battle in the marketplace do
not mention the Quetzal-Owl at all. This magical symbol of
Mexica power and tradition meant nothing to the Spaniards.

On August 13, 1521, the Spanish forces easily broke
through the Mexica's last defenses at Tlatelolco. Even though
all hope was gone, Cuauhtemoc did not surrender. Instead, he
attempted to leave the city by canoe, accompanied by his family
and close advisers. One of the Spanish brigantines overtook the
canoes, and the last emperor of the Mexica was captured.

*In this painting from the Conquest of Mexico series, Spanish soldiers
have captured the emperor Cuauhtemoc in his canoe. Brigantines
with their sails can be seen in the background.*

López de Gómara described the meeting between the triumphant Cortés and the defeated emperor. Cuauhtemoc said, "I have done everything in my power to defend myself and my people, and everything that it was my duty to do." He reached out and touched the dagger that Cortés wore on his belt, saying "You may do with me whatever you wish, so kill me, for that would be best." Cortés did not kill the Mexica ruler but instead "comforted him with kind words and the hope of life and authority."

After the capture of Cuauhtemoc, the fighting ceased and silence fell over Tenochtitlan. The long and terrible war between the Spaniards and the Mexica was finally over.

AFTER THE FALL

After the final Spanish victory, the city of Tenochtitlan was a desolate place. Its streets and canals were filled with the bodies of Mexica people who had been killed in battle or died from starvation. Those who were still alive fled from the city, some in canoes across the lake, others along the causeways. "The grownups carried their young children on the shoulders," says the *Florentine Codex*. "Many of the children were weeping with terror, but a few of them laughed . . . thinking it was great sport to be carried like that along the road."

Amid the wreckage of Tenochtitlan, the victorious Spaniards searched for gold. They stopped the fleeing refugees, looking under the skirts of the women and the men's loincloths for objects made of the precious metal. Cortés ordered Cuauhtemoc to bring him all the gold in the Mexica treasury. He even demanded the gold bars lost during the Spanish flight from the city in 1519.

When the Mexica could not provide the gold demanded, the Spaniards used more drastic means. According to several Spanish accounts (including that of López de Gómara), Cortés had Cuauhtemoc tortured to force him to reveal where the Mexica treasures were hidden. The emperor's feet were dipped in oil and held over a fire. López de Gómara said that Cortés eventually stopped the torture "either because he thought it degrading and cruel, or because [Cuauhtemoc] had told him that, ten days before his capture, . . . he had thrown . . . his gold and silver, precious stones, . . . and rich jewels into the water."

Cortés sent men to search in the canals, but he never found the treasures of gold that he sought. He ordered his native allies to remove the bodies in the city and to repair the bridges and causeways. The aqueduct was restored, and water once more flowed into Tenochtitlan. But for the Mexica people, nothing would ever be the same.

Broken spears lie in the roads;
we have torn our hair in our grief.
The houses are roofless now, and their walls
are red with blood. . . .

We have pounded our hands in despair
against the adobe walls,
for our inheritance, our city, is lost and dead.
The shields of our warriors were its defense,
but they could not save it.

—*Cantares Mexicanos*

CHAPTER EIGHT
MEXICO BECOMES NEW SPAIN

From all I have seen and understood touching the
similarity between this land and that of Spain, . . . it
seemed to me that the most suitable name for it was
New Spain. . . . I humbly entreat Your Highness to
look favorably on this and order it to be so called.

—*Hernán Cortés, Second Letter from Mexico, 1520*

After the fall of Tenochtitlan, Hernán Cortés began the
process that would turn the empire of the Mexica into His
Majesty's province of New Spain. As a first step, Cortés
sent out his captains to take control of areas outside central
Mexico. Cristóbal de Olid led his army to Michoacan and
later Honduras to bring the native people under Spanish
rule. Pedro de Alvarado went to the area that is modern-day
Guatemala, inhabited by the descendants of the Maya. Ten

Cortes studies plans for the construction of Mexico City while a priest and another Spaniard look on.

years after the Mexica conquest, most of this territory was part of New Spain.

The new Spanish province needed a capital, and Cortés decided to build it on the ruins of the Mexica capital, Tenochtitlan. According to López de Gómara, Cortés decided "to rebuild Mexico [Tenochtitlan], not so much because of the majestic situation of the city, as because of its fame and renown; also because he wanted to repair the damage he had done."

Repair was hardly possible, however, given the destruction of the city. With the help of the Tlaxcalans and other native allies, the surviving buildings were leveled, and new Spanish structures were built on top of the rubble. Cortés's grand residence was located on the site of Motecuzoma's palace. The great central square of Tenochtitlan became the main plaza of the new provincial capital, which would be called Mexico City. Eventually, a large Roman Catholic cathedral was erected near the site of the great pyramid that had held the temples of Huitzilopochtli and Tlaloc.

While Mexico City was under construction, Cortés made his headquarters in the city of Coyohuacan, which had not been destroyed during the conquest. From there he maintained control over the land he had conquered. In 1521 he had written to the king of Spain, telling him about the conquest of the Mexica and asking to be put in charge of the new territory. There was political turmoil in Spain at the time, however, and the king and his advisers sent no reply. Cortés finally received his official appointment as captain-general of New Spain in 1523, but by then, he had already made many decisions about the future of the new territory.

One thing that Cortés had done was to give encomiendas to Alvarado, Olid, Sandoval, and all the other men who had fought with him. Instead of the gold treasures they had hoped for, his followers were given pieces of land and the right to use the labor of people living on it. The encomienda system, common in the Spanish Caribbean, became the basis for land ownership in large parts of Mexico. The towns and territories once controlled by native rulers were put into the hands of Spanish *encomanderos*. Instead of producing tribute goods for the Mexica, the common people of Mexico raised crops, tended animals, and mined gold and silver for the Spaniards.

ENCOMIENDAS

In thickly populated central Mexico, the encomiendas assigned to the Spaniards were often in cities and towns. Pedro de Alvarado received the town of Xochimilco and its population to provide him services and income. Cortés held Coyohuacan, Chalco, and two other communities. Even some high-ranking Mexica were granted encomiendas. One of Motecuzoma's sons, who became the Christian gentleman known as Don Pedro, received Tula, the ancient capital of the Toltecs, for his use.

IMPORTED FROM EUROPE

Many of the crops and animals raised on the Spanish encomiendas were previously unknown to the people of Mexico. Maize, tomatoes, peppers, beans, potatoes, avocados, and squash had all originated in the Americas. The Spaniards introduced a whole new range of European food plants, including wheat, barley, and many kinds of fruits. Cattle, sheep, pigs, and chickens also made their appearance in a land that previously had almost no domesticated animals.

These imports from Europe caused tremendous changes in Mexico, some of which were beneficial. Pigs and chickens provided easily available sources of protein in the diet of the common people. Wool from the Spanish merino sheep could be used to supplement the native fibers of cotton and agave. The introduction of horses, oxen, and donkeys made transportation of goods and people easier.

Some of the changes caused by the introduction of European plants and animals were not so favorable.

This illustration from the Florentine Codex shows farmers harvesting, threshing, and storing grain.

The Spaniards preferred wheat bread to tortillas made of maize, but wheat was a much more difficult crop to raise. It took more labor and needed more water than corn. Another plant that the Spaniards introduced to Mexico was sugarcane, which was native to the Caribbean islands. Processed into sugar, it was a cash crop for the Spaniards, but like wheat, it required intensive cultivation. Valuable agricultural land was used to grow these European crops, and laborers on the encomiendas worked to produce wheat and sugar instead of growing their own staple crop, maize.

The large numbers of cattle and sheep that the Spaniards brought to Mexico destroyed fields of native crops and damaged the land by overgrazing. They ate the protective ground cover that retained moisture, and large areas of land in central Mexico became dry and unproductive.

MEXICAN ANIMALS

Before the conquest, the Mexica had many domesticated plants but few animals—only turkeys, dogs, and honeybees. Large animals such as horses, oxen, and the llamas found in South America were not native to Mexico. Because of this, the Mexica did not have domesticated animals to plow fields or transport goods.

The new crops and animals were a mixed blessing for the people of Mexico, but other European imports were totally destructive. These were the diseases that the Spaniards unknowingly brought with them to the new lands. The smallpox epidemic that had weakened the Mexica in 1521 was only the first in a wave of epidemics that swept over New Spain. In the early 1530s, measles killed thousands. An epidemic that was either typhus or influenza struck in 1545 and ravaged the population for three years. Another deadly epidemic occurred between 1576 and 1581.

As a result of what was called the Great Dying, the number of native people in Mexico declined drastically. Many historians believe that the population at the end of the 1500s was 40 to 50 percent less than when the Spaniards first arrived. A few claim that as much as 95 percent of the native population died from European diseases.

The effects of this population decline were felt all over Mexico. Empty of inhabitants, whole towns and villages were abandoned. In other areas, the loss of community leaders destroyed the social network that supported the common people. These changes made it easier for the Spaniards to control New Spain and to set up their own political and social systems. European diseases completed the conquest of Mexico that had begun with Cortés's defeat of the Mexica in 1521.

A GREAT HARVEST

Another import from Europe, the Christian religion, also caused great change in Mexico. Beginning with Columbus, Spanish explorers had been determined to bring Christianity to the New World. In his fourth letter to the king, Cortés told His Highness "of the readiness displayed by some of the natives of these parts to be converted to Our Holy Catholic Faith and to become Christians." He requested that His Holy Majesty "should send . . . many religious persons . . . who would be most zealous in the conversion of these people."

Roman Catholic missionaries began to arrive in Mexico as early as 1523. Most were members of religious orders dedicated to teaching and preaching the gospel, such as the Franciscans and Dominicans. Believing sincerely in their own faith and horrified by the "idols" and ceremonies of the Mexica religion, these zealous men set about converting the native people. "As soon as the friars arrived, the work of conversion was actively undertaken," said López de Gómara. "The idols were cast down, and . . . a great harvest of teaching, baptizing, and marrying was reaped."

To wipe out all memory of the native religion, the missionaries decided to destroy the Mexica's books. To their eyes, these documents filled with strange symbols and pictures were all works of the devil. Some of the Mexica books, or codices, did record religious rituals and stories,

yemoquayateq
que tlatoque

Roman Catholic missionaries brought Christianity to the people of
New Spain. This drawing from the Lienzo de Tlaxcala shows a priest
celebrating Mass.

but many others contained histories, calendars, tax records,
and other ordinary information. Almost all of these ancient
documents were burned. Only about twenty have survived.

The missionaries worked tirelessly to replace the old
Mexica religion with the Roman Catholic faith. They
learned Nahuatl and other native languages so that they
could preach the Christian gospel to the native people.
Missionary orders built churches and monasteries throughout
central Mexico. Education was an important tool of
conversion, and the missionaries established schools where
young Mexicans, particularly those from the upper class,
could learn Spanish and receive a Christian education.

In the years following the conquest of the Mexica, many native people became Christians. Toribio de Benavente, a Franciscan friar also known as Motolinia, claimed that by 1537 as many as nine million had been baptized, four million by members of his own order. These numbers are probably exaggerated, but the success of the missionaries was undeniable.

Whether the converted people understood or fully accepted their new religion is another question. In some respects, the Roman Catholic faith blended with elements of the old religion. Christian saints took on the attributes of the Mexica gods of nature. Old religious rituals—for example, dancing—were sometimes combined with church services. Human sacrifice, of course, was strictly forbidden.

In New Spain, religion was as much a part of everyday life as it had been before the conquest. The holy days of the Catholic Church took the place of the many festivals on the Mexica religious calendar. Only the gods and the ceremonies were different.

WHO RULES NEW SPAIN?

After his appointment as captain-general and governor in 1523, Cortés ruled New Spain as if he were a king. He dressed in black silk and was always "surrounded by a large number of servants, . . . attendants, stewards, secretaries, valets, . . . chaplains, treasurers, and all such." Wherever Cortés passed by, the native people prostrated themselves before him, just as they had done with Motecuzoma.

Despite his exalted position, Cortés insisted that he

was only a representative of the Spanish king and had no desire to rule Mexico on his own. Others doubted this claim, however. Cortés had many enemies in Spain, and they tried to convince the king that the conqueror was becoming too powerful. Although King Charles had appointed Cortés governor, he too was concerned about the extent of Cortés's influence. The king sent Spanish court officials to New Spain to keep an eye on Cortés's actions.

In 1524 Cortés left Mexico City to lead an expedition to Honduras to capture his old comrade Cristóbal de Olid. After conquering that region, Olid had set himself up as ruler, in defiance of Cortés's orders. Olid's accomplice in this plot was none other than the Cuban governor Diego Velásquez, whose orders Cortés had ignored in 1519.

The expedition to Honduras started out as a great adventure, with jugglers, dancers, and musicians accompanying an army of several thousand men. Also included in the company were many Mexica nobles, among them the emperor Cuauhtemoc, who was still a prisoner. Cortés brought the nobles along so that they could not plan a rebellion while he was away from Mexico City.

What started out as an adventure soon turned into a nightmare, as Cortés and his men struggled through wild and uncharted land. In his biography of Cortés, López de Gómara gives a vivid account of the journey. "Cortés crossed a swamp half a league wide, and then a deep estuary, over which he had to construct a bridge; and farther on, another swamp. . . . [The Spaniards] were now in such a dense forest that they could see only the sky above them and the ground they trod. . . . They wandered about lost in it for two days."

During the difficult journey to Honduras, Cuauhtemoc and the other Mexica lords were accused of plotting to kill Cortés. They were tried, found guilty, and sentenced to death. The last emperor of the Mexica was hanged from the branches of a large ceiba tree in 1525. Writing of his death, López de Gómara described Cuauhtemoc as "a valiant man [who] in every adversity proved his royal heart and courage."

When the expedition finally reached Honduras, Cortés learned that Olid had already been captured and executed by officers who had come from Mexico by sea. He had made the disastrous trip for nothing. Returning by ship in 1526, Cortés found Mexico City in chaos. Assuming that Cortés had died in Honduras, the king's officials and his own followers were engaged in a struggle for power. Cortés was able to regain control, but his authority and his reputation had been severely damaged.

RETURN TO SPAIN

In 1528 Cortés went to Spain to ask for the support of King Charles. He traveled "as a great lord," said López de Gómara, taking with him "a son of Moctezuma . . . and many gentlemen and lords of Mexico, Tlaxcala, and other cities." Also along on the trip was Cortés's own son, Martín, who had been born to the interpreter Malinche in 1522.

The people of Spain were eager to meet the conqueror of Mexico. "The whole kingdom was agog with his fame . . . , and everyone wanted to see him." Charles gave Cortés a very cordial welcome, and "in recognition of his services and the worth of his person, made him Marques del Valle de Oaxaca," a title that Cortés had requested.

Cortés had received a very cordial reception from the king, and Cortés hoped that his position in Mexico would be improved. But he had another, more personal, reason for coming to Spain. He needed a wife. Cortés's first wife, Catalina, had died in 1522, and his friends in Spain had been looking for a suitable replacement. They arranged a match between Cortés and Doña Juana de Zuñiga, a beautiful woman from a wealthy and aristocratic family.

Despite the honors bestowed on him by the king, Cortés never regained his power in Mexico. After his return in 1529, he spent most of his time in legal disputes. Although Cortés still had the title of captain-general, the real government of New Spain was in the hands of viceroys, who were direct representatives of the Spanish king. Antonio de Mendoza, who became viceroy in 1535, was a capable

CATALINA'S DEATH

In 1526 a judge was sent from Spain to hold a commission of inquiry, called a *residencia*, against Cortés. One of the many accusations brought before the commission was that Cortés had murdered his first wife, Catalina Suárez. Catalina had come to Mexico in 1522 and died several months later under mysterious circumstances. Many witnesses came forward to testify that Cortés had strangled or smothered his wife. The charges against him were eventually dropped, but the truth about Catalina's death remained a mystery.

administrator who made sure that Cortés's power and influence were strictly limited.

Cortés, frustrated and bored with his life in New Spain, turned again to exploration. He sent out expeditions to explore Mexico's Pacific Coast and to search for a strait that connected the Pacific with the Caribbean Sea. (Of course, there was no such connection until the Panama Canal was opened in 1914.) In 1535 Cortés himself sailed north into the Gulf of California, then called the Sea of Cortés. The trip was a disaster. Ships ran aground and had to be abandoned, and their crews almost starved.

The expeditions Cortés had sponsored made no important new discoveries, and they had cost a lot of money. López de Gómara said that "no one ever spent so much and so zealously in such enterprises."

In 1540 Cortés returned again to Spain to seek the king's support. He was forty-six years old and eager to prove that he was still a man of courage and action. In the following year, he joined King Charles's campaign against Algerian pirates who were attacking ships in the Mediterranean Sea. The Spanish fleet was shipwrecked, and Cortés lost all the gold he carried with him, as well as five precious emeralds given to him in Mexico. "The war turned out to be more costly for him than anyone except His Majesty," López de Gómara commented.

DEATH OF A CONQUEROR

Cortés never again returned to the land he had conquered. His final years were spent in Spain, where he lived in a town near Seville with his wife, Doña Juana, and their four children. After a long illness, he died on December 2, 1547, at the age of sixty-three. His son by Doña Juana, also named Martín, inherited his estate and the title of Marques del Valle. His daughters were given good dowries.

According to López de Gómara, Cortés had several illegitimate children. In addition to Martín, Malinche's son, he also had a son by a Spanish woman and "three daughters, each by a different mother, all Indians." In his will, he provided for the support of these children and also left money to establish a school and a hospital in Mexico City. He requested that his body be buried at the hospital. In the final pages of his biography, López de Gómara described Cortés in these words:

> He was very strong, courageous, and skillful at arms. As a youth, he was mischievous; as a man, serene; . . . he was always a leader in war as well as in peace. . . . He was much give to consorting with women . . . a very stubborn man, as a result of which he had more lawsuits that was proper to his station. He spent liberally on war, women, friends, and fancies. . . . He was devout and given to praying; . . . a great giver of alms. . . . Such, just as you have heard, was Cortés, Conqueror of New Spain.

VICTORS AND VANQUISHED

> The history of European expansion includes few stories
> of drama and tragedy equal to the Spanish conquest
> of Mexico and the fall of the great indigenous [native]
> empire that controlled its heartland.
>
> —*Stuart Schwartz*, Victors and Vanquished, 2000

In 1492, as everyone knows, Christopher Columbus "discovered" a new world completely unknown to Europeans. The Caribbean islands where he first landed were inhabited by people who lived simple lives. They had few possessions and only the most basic kind of government. Columbus and the Spaniards who followed him quickly took control of the islands and forced the native people to do their bidding.

When Hernán Cortés arrived in Mexico in 1519, he found a very different kind of native society. The people lived in large towns and cities. They practiced a complex religion and had an elaborate social system, made up of different classes and occupations. A strong central government, backed by a large and powerful army, controlled the territory and the lives of the people.

Conquering this kind of highly developed society was not as easy as overcoming the people of the Caribbean islands. Using all their resources, the Mexica fought against the foreigners who had invaded their land. The battle was long and fierce, but the outcome was the same. The Europeans were the victors, and the native people were the vanquished.

European domination of the Americas began with the conquest of Mexico. Other conquests soon followed. In 1532 another Spaniard, Francisco Pizarro, defeated the powerful Inca Empire of Peru. During the following years, Spain and Portugal established outposts in many parts of South America. It was not until the 1600s that Europeans made their way to the shores of North America. The English who settled in Jamestown in 1607 were not conquerors, but their intrusion marked the end of native rule just as surely as Cortés's defeat of the Mexica.

The European conquests brought about "world-shattering changes" that transformed the lives of native people in the Americas. The natural course of their history and development was abruptly ended. What would have happened to the Mexica empire if Cortés had not shown up? Would it have crumbled under pressure from its many enemies? Would a strong ruler have united the empire and led it to greater glory? No one will ever know.

THE CONQUEROR'S TOMB

There are very few monuments to Hernán Cortés in modern Mexico. Although the conqueror is buried in Mexico City, few know the location of his tomb. Immediately after his death, Cortés was buried in a village church near Seville, Spain. In 1566 his remains were taken to Mexico and placed in a church in Texcoco. During the following years, the conqueror's bones were moved to various different locations. Finally, in 1794, they were entombed in the Hospital de Jesús Nazareno in Mexico City, which Cortés had established in his will. In 1981 the Mexican government moved the body to an undisclosed location in the city because of threats from people who wanted to destroy the conqueror's remains.

AN END AND A BEGINNING

The "world-shattering changes" that began with the conquest of Mexico eventually led to the creation of another world, one that still exists. In the words of a modern historian, "The fall of Tenochtitlan signaled both an end and a beginning."

The son born to Malinche and Cortés was the first child of that new world, and many others followed. Unions between Spaniards and the native Mexicans created a new people of mixed ancestry and heritage. Spanish became the dominant language in Mexico, but many native languages survived. Nahuatl, the language of the Mexica, is still spoken in modern Mexico. If you visit the Zocalo, the main square in Mexico City, you can see not only the Roman Catholic

Cathedral but also the ruins of the Great Pyramid and the temple of Huitzilopochtli, which have been excavated and carefully restored. In the land of the Mexica, the past has not been forgotten.

> They were our grandfathers, our grandmothers. . . .
> Their account was repeated,
> they left it to us; . . .
> to us who live now,
> to us who come down from them.
> Never will it be lost, never will it be forgotten.

> —*Crónica Mexicayotl* (A chronicle of the Mexica)

The ruins of the Mexica Great Pyramid are restored in downtown Mexico City.

PRIMARY SOURCE RESEARCH

To learn about historical events, people study many sources, such as books, websites, newspaper articles, photographs, and paintings. These sources can be separated into two general categories—primary sources and secondary sources.

A primary source is the record of an eyewitness. Primary sources provide firsthand accounts about a person or event. Examples include diaries, letters, autobiographies, speeches, newspapers, and oral history interviews. Libraries, archives, historical societies, and museums often have primary sources available on-site or on the Internet.

A secondary source is published information that was researched, collected, and written or otherwise created by someone who was not an eyewitness. These authors or artists use primary sources and other secondary sources in their research, but they interpret and arrange the source material in their own works. Secondary sources include history books, novels, biographies, movies, documentaries, and magazines. Libraries and museums are filled with secondary sources.

After finding primary and secondary sources, authors and historians must evaluate them. They may ask questions such as: Who created this document? What is this person's point of view? What biases might this person have? How trustworthy is this document? Just because a person was an eyewitness to an event does not mean that person recorded the whole truth about that event. For example, a soldier describing a battle might depict only the heroic actions of his unit and only the brutal behavior of the enemy. An account from a soldier on the opposing side might portray the same battle very differently. When sources disagree, researchers must decide through additional study which explanation makes the most sense. For this reason, historians consult a variety of primary and secondary sources. Then they can draw their own conclusions.

The Pivotal Moments in History series takes readers on a journey to important junctures in history that shaped our modern world. Authors research each event using both primary and secondary sources, an approach that enhances readers' awareness of the complexities of the materials and helps bring to life the rich stories from which we draw our understanding of our shared history.

PRIMARY SOURCE DOCUMENTS

In researching a subject, historians rely on eyewitness accounts to learn the "true" story of a past event or period. For the Spanish conquest of Mexico, researchers have three major sources, each with its own unique background and point of view.

One of these eyewitness accounts comes from Hernán Cortés, who led the Spanish forces against the native people of Mexico. Cortés's letters to the Spanish king Charles, written during the period from 1519 to 1524, describe in great detail the conqueror's experiences in Mexico. Three of the five letters were printed and published in Europe during the 1520s.

They were very popular among readers who were fascinated by accounts of the New World. There are no surviving copies of Cortés's first letter, presumably written in 1519.

In his letters to King Charles, Cortés presents a historical record of his travels in Mexico, the battles he fought, and the victories he won. His reasons for writing, however, were as much political as they were historical. He wanted to convince the king to support his actions and to take his side against Diego Velásquez, the governor of Cuba who opposed Cortés. He also hoped that King Charles, "His Holy Majesty, Most Powerful Lord," would appoint him as ruler of the land he had conquered. In the letters, Cortés emphasized his own leadership role during the conquest and his loyalty and devotion to the king.

Another important eyewitness account is that of Bernal Díaz del Castillo, a Spaniard who was with Cortés throughout his time in Mexico. Díaz wrote his book, *The True History of the Conquest of New Spain*, in the 1560s, when he was an old man in his seventies. It was not published until 1632. Díaz's writing is very different from Cortés's smooth and elegant prose. His book is a long and rambling story told by an old soldier remembering his exciting past. But what a story it is! In a blunt and straightforward style, Díaz describes fascinating details about what he saw in Mexico—the markets, the temples, and the clothes and appearance of the native people. He also gives vivid accounts of his own experiences as a foot soldier in Cortés's army.

Like Cortés, however, Bernal Díaz del Castillo did not write his book only as a historical record. He had other motives. Díaz believed that Cortés's letters and other published accounts of the conquest did not tell the real story of what happened in Mexico. He was particularly disturbed by a biography of Hernán Cortés, published in 1552. The book's author, Francisco López de Gómara, had never been to Mexico. He was a scholar who had served as Cortés's secretary after the conqueror returned to Spain. Díaz believed that López de Gómara had given Cortés too much credit for the defeat of the Mexica and had ignored the contributions of ordinary Spanish soldiers like himself. His own book, *The True History of the Conquest of New Spain*, was meant to set the record straight.

A third major eyewitness account of the conquest represents the Mexica point of view. It is part of a very important document from the 1550s known as the *Florentine Codex*. Book 12 of the codex, titled "The War of Conquest: How It Was Waged Here in Mexico," is based on interviews with Mexica people conducted by the Spanish friar Bernardino de Sahagún during the 1540s and 1550s. Many of the men interviewed had fought against the Spaniards during the final assault on Tenochtitlan and were able to give detailed descriptions of the conflict. They also described events such as the attack at the festival of Toxcatl and the behavior of Cortés, Motecuzoma, and other major figures.

The *Florentine Codex* is essential in understanding the conquest of Mexico, but like the Spanish sources, it has to be seen in relation to its background and origins. In collecting information for the codex, Sahagún worked with young Mexica men who had been converted to Christianity and had learned Spanish. These assistants conducted interviews with Mexica people in three different locations: Tenochtitlan, Tlatelolco, and a city called Tepepulco. The information they gathered was recorded in Nahuatl using the Latin alphabet and then translated into Spanish by Sahagún.

The result is an amazing historical document, considered one of the first works of anthropological research. Since Friar Bernardino de Sahagún's research was done almost thirty years after the conquest, however, some historians question its reliability as an eyewitness account. They wonder how much the viewpoint of the informants and the interviewers had been affected by the years of Spanish colonial rule and the influence of the Roman Catholic Church. Were their memories of the conquest accurate, or had they been reinterpreted in light of later experiences that had so drastically changed their lives?

There are other questions about the "eyewitness" accounts presented in the *Florentine Codex*. Many of Sahagún's informants came from Tlatelolco, a city that had been in conflict with Tenochtitlan for many years. The information that they provided may have been biased against their old enemy and particularly against Motecuzoma. Another issue is Bernardino de Sahagún's interpretation of the native accounts he had collected. Did he add his own views in an attempt to explain the Mexica and their history?

Despite such questions, the *Florentine Codex* remains an extremely valuable resource in learning about the Spanish conquest of Mexico. It is the only major primary source that presents the story from a native point of view, even though that view may be distorted by outside influences.

By studying the *Florentine Codex* along with the accounts of Hernán Cortés and Bernal Díaz del Castillo, we can begin to understand this extremely important historical event.

INTERPRETING THE PAST

The translator Malinche is an important figure in the history of the Spanish Conquest, but just what role did she play? Was Malinche a heroic character or was she a villain and a traitor? It all depends on your point of view.

Hernán Cortés and his biographer, Francisco López de Gómara, say little about Malinche's part in the conquest, but Bernal Díaz del Castillo speaks of her often and always with affection and admiration. In his book, he calls her respectfully Doña Marina and praises her skills as a translator. Díaz describes Malinche as a talented woman who used her own knowledge and intelligence in negotiating with the Mexica on Cortés's behalf.

When Malinche is mentioned in native accounts, she also receives favorable treatment. The interpreter is often referred to as Malintzin. The last syllable of the name, *tzin*, is a respectful title in the Nahuatl language, similar to the Spanish *Doña*. In native drawings of the conquest—for example, those in the *Florentine Codex*—Malinche is featured prominently. In the *Lienzo de Tlaxcala*, a series of drawings commissioned by the city of the Tlaxcala in 1552, she is shown as a dignified woman with flowing hair, standing at Cortés's side as he confronts Motecuzoma and other native rulers.

In this illustration from the Lienzo de Tlaxcala, *Malinche (center) is shown translating for Cortés. To indicate Malinche's importance, the artist has made her the largest and most imposing figure in the scene.*

These favorable portrayals of Malinche were common after the conquest and during the colonial period in Mexico. When Mexico won its independence from Spain in 1821, however, everything changed. Malinche came to be seen not as an admirable figure but as a despised traitor. The nationalists who had won the revolution against Spain rejected Mexico's colonial past and the conquest that had made it possible. Because Malinche had aided the conquerors, she was viewed as a traitor who had betrayed her own people. Her name was even used to create a word, *malinchista*, meaning "someone who rejects his or her native heritage." Writers of the period condemned Malinche not only as a traitor but also as an immoral woman because she was Cortés's mistress and had a child by him.

Many modern historians believe that these accusations are inaccurate and unfair. Malinche did not betray the people of Mexico. At the time of the conquest, there was no Mexican nation, only different cities and ethnic groups that were in constant conflict with one another. Although she spoke Nahuatl, Malinche was not a Mexica. Her own people had sold her as a slave to the Maya, who then gave her to the Spaniards. To whom did she owe her loyalty?

Like most women of her time, Malinche was not free to decide what she would or would not do. She did not choose to work for Cortés or to become his mistress. Others made that decision for her. Once the situation had been forced on her, however, Malinche did what she had to do to survive. She used her abilities as an interpreter and her natural intelligence to make a place for herself in a world that offered few options for women. Malinche was neither a hero nor a traitor but an individual dealing with the circumstances that life had handed her.

TIMELINE

1200   The Mexica settle in the Valley of Mexico.

1345   Tenochtitlan, the Mexica capital, is built on a rocky island in Lake Texcoco.

1440   Motecuzoma I becomes tlatoani and expands Mexica territory.

1469   Isabella, princess of the Spanish kingdom of Castile, marries Ferdinand, prince of Aragon.

1485   Hernán Cortés is born in Medellin, Spain.

1492   The Moorish city of Granada is defeated by the armies of Christian Spain in January. Christopher Columbus sails the Atlantic and lands on the Caribbean island of San Salvador in November.

1496   Bernal Díaz del Castillo is born in Medina del Campo, Spain.

1502   A Spanish colony is established on the island of Hispaniola. Motecuzoma II becomes tlatoani of the Mexica kingdom.

1503   Cortés arrives in Hispaniola.

1511   Diego Velásquez establishes a colony in Cuba. He becomes governor, with Cortés as his secretary.

1515   Cortés marries Catalina Suárez.

1517	Francisco Hernández de Córdoba leads an expedition to Yucatán, Mexico.
1518	Juan de Grijalva leads a second expedition to Yucatán.
1519	An expedition led by Cortés reaches Yucatán in March. Cortes establishes the town of Vera Cruz. In July, Cortés disables expedition ships, preventing their return to Cuba. In September a battle between Spaniards and Tlaxcalans occurs and Tlaxcala becomes an ally. In October, Spaniards kill nobles in Cholula. Cortés and his forces enter Tenochtitlan on November 8. Motecuzoma is taken prisoner on November 11.
1520	The Narváez expedition sent by Velásquez reaches Mexico in April with orders to capture Cortés. In early May, Cortés confronts Narváez and defeats him in battle. In mid-May, Pedro de Alvarado orders the massacre of the Mexica at the festival of Toxcatl. Cortés returns to Tenochtitlan on June 24. On June 29, Motecuzoma is killed and Cuitlahuac becomes tlatoani. On June 30, Spaniards flee Tenochtitlan—La Noche Triste. In October a smallpox epidemic strikes Tenochtitlan. Tlatoani Cuitlahuac dies on December 4. Cortés and his allies leave Tlaxcala on December 29 for a final attack on Tenochtitlan.

1521	Cuauhtemoc become tlatoani in February. Cortés attacks cities around Lake Texcoco in April and gains more allies. Forces of Alvarado, Sandoval, and Olid begin an assault on Tenochtitlan on May 22. On May 26, Spaniards destroy the aqueduct from Chapultepec, cutting off the water supply. On May 30, Spaniards in brigantines enter the lake and engage in battle with Mexica who are in canoes. From June 10 to 15, Cortés leads an attack into the heart of the city. On June 30, the Mexica defeat the Spaniards in battle in Tlatelolco and sacrifice sixty-eight Spanish captives. Spaniards push back Mexica forces in July. On July 27, Spaniards burn the temple in Tlatelolco. In early August, fierce fighting occurs in Tlatelolco. Cuauhtemoc sends out the Quetzal-Owl warrior. On August 13, Cuauhtemoc is captured and Tenochtitlan surrenders.
1521–1522	Mexico becomes a colony of New Spain. Mexico City is built on ruins of Tenochtitlan.
1522	The first Roman Catholic missionaries arrive in New Spain.
1523	Cortés is appointed captain-general of New Spain.
1525	Cortés leads an expedition to Honduras, taking Cuauhtemoc with him. Cuauhtemoc is accused of rebellion and executed.

1528	Cortés goes to Spain, marries Doña Juana de Zuñiga, and receives the title of Marques del Valle.
1529	Cortés returns to Mexico and sends out expeditions to explore new territory.
1540	Cortés returns to Spain. He joins the king's campaign against Algerian pirates.
1547	Hernán Cortés dies in a town near Seville, Spain.
1552	A biography of Cortés by Francisco López de Gómara is published.
1584	Bernal Díaz del Castillo dies on his encomienda in Guatemala.
1632	Díaz's book, *The True History of the Conquest of New Spain*, is published.

GLOSSARY

ALCALDE: a magistrate of a community, similar to a mayor

ATLATL: a device made of wood or bone used to throw spears and darts

AZTLAN: the legendary homeland of the Mexica people before they settled in the Valley of Mexico. The name *Aztec* comes from this word.

BRIGANTINE: a small, easily maneuvered sailing ship equipped with both sails and oars

CALMECAC: a Mexica school for upper-class children. Future priests and military and political leaders received their education in calmecacs.

CALPULLI (PL. CALPULTIN): a social unit in a Mexica city made up of groups of families who lived in a specific district

CHINAMPA: a small plot of agricultural land formed by piling soil onto a platform of logs and branches. Some chinampas floated freely in Lake Texcoco, while others were attached to the lake bottom.

CIHUACOATL: a high-ranking Mexica official who held a position similar to a vice president or prime minister

ENCOMIENDA: a grant giving Spaniards the right to use the labor of a certain number of native people living in a specific area. The *encomandero* (the individual receiving the grant) was responsible for the physical and spiritual welfare of the laborers.

HIDALGO: a Spanish nobleman of low rank

MACEHUALTIN: the lower class of Mexica people

PILLI (PL. PIPILTIN): a member of the Mexica upper class; a noble

POCHTECA: Mexica merchants who engaged in long-distance trade

RECONQUISTA: the defeat, or reconquest, of the Moorish kingdoms in Spain

REQUERIMIENTO: a legal document declaring that all the native people of the Americas owed their loyalty to the king of Spain and the Roman Catholic pope

RESIDENCIA: a legal inquiry into the conduct of a Spanish official

TLATOANI: the title of the Mexica ruler, meaning "speaker," or "he who says something"

VICEROY: a direct representative of the king (*roy* in old Spanish) who governs a colony

WHO'S WHO?

GERÓNIMO DE AGUILAR (CA. 1481–1539) A Spaniard who had been shipwrecked off the coast of Yucatán in 1511, Aguilar was captured by the Maya and learned the local language. He served as a translator for Cortés while the expedition was in Maya territory and later worked with Malinche in translating Nahuatl into Maya and then Spanish.

PEDRO DE ALVARADO (1485–1541) Alvarado came to Cuba in 1510 and was a member of the first expedition to Yucatán. He joined Cortés in 1519. Alvarado gave the order for the massacre at the Toxcatl festival. After the fall of Tenochtitlan, he led Spanish forces in conquering Guatemala and became its first governor. Alvarado died from injuries received when he fell off his horse during a military campaign in northern Mexico.

CACAMA (1483–1520) The king of Texcoco and Motecuzoma's nephew, Cacama was killed by the Spaniards in 1520, during the conflict following the Toxcatl massacre.

144

CHARLES V (1500–1558) The grandson of Isabella and Ferdinand, Charles was king of Spain from 1516 to 1556 and Holy Roman Emperor from 1519 to 1556. His father, Philip, was a member of the royal Hapsburg family of Austria, and Charles inherited the imperial throne of the Holy Roman Empire through him.

MARTÍN CORTÉS (1522–? AND 1532–?) Two sons of Hernán Cortés were named Martín. The mother of the older Martín was the native woman Malinche. He was born in 1522 and sent to Spain at an early age, where he became a page in the Spanish royal court. The younger Martín, born in 1532, was Cortés's legitimate son by his second wife, Doña Juana de Zuñiga. He inherited his father's estate and his title of Marques del Valle.

CUAUHTEMOC (CA. 1495–1525) The last ruler of the Mexica empire, he was the son of the emperor Ahuitzotl and a nephew of Motecuzoma. Cuauhtemoc led the Mexica defense against the Spaniards and refused to surrender Tenochtitlan. He was captured in August 1519 and executed by Cortés in 1525.

CUITLAHUAC (?–1520) A brother of Motecuzoma, Cuitlahuac took the throne after his death and ruled for only eighty days. He died in the smallpox epidemic of 1520.

BERNAL DÍAZ DEL CASTILLO (1495–1583) Arriving from Spain in 1514, Díaz del Castillo was a member of the Grijalva expedition. He returned to Mexico with Cortés in 1519 and was with him throughout the conquest period. After the fall of Tenochtitlan, Díaz fought with Alvarado in Guatemala and received an encomienda there. He wrote his famous book during the 1550s and 1560s in response to López de Gómara's biography glorifying Cortés. The book was published in 1632.

JUAN DE GRIJALVA (CA. 1480–1527) A nephew of Governor Diego Velásquez, Grijalva led an expedition to Yucatán in 1518.

FRANCISCO LÓPEZ DE GÓMARA (1511–1566) A priest and distinguished scholar, López de Gómara became Cortés's secretary when the conqueror returned to Spain in 1540. He wrote his biography based on Cortés's letters, personal documents, and stories of his years in Mexico.

MALINCHE (?–1551) Sold as a slave to the Maya, Malinche spoke a dialect of the Maya language and Nahuatl, the language of the Mexica. When she was given to Cortés as a gift, he employed her as a translator and relied on her skills throughout his time in Mexico. Malinche was also Cortés's mistress and had a son by him. In 1525 she married Juan Jaramillo, one of Cortés's military commanders.

MOTECUZOMA II (CA. 1468–1520) The sixth ruler of the Mexica empire, Motecuzoma came to the throne in 1502 after serving as a distinguished military leader and a member of the emperor's council. His reluctance to resist the Spanish invaders in 1519 made him very unpopular with the Mexica. According to Spanish reports, Motecuzoma was killed by his own people after the Toxcatl massacre.

PÁNFILO DE NARVÁEZ (CA. 1480–1528) Narváez commanded a fleet sent by Diego Velásquez to capture Cortés and bring him back to Cuba. When Narváez landed on the Mexican coast in April 1520, Cortés defeated his army and took him prisoner.

CRISTÓBAL DE OLID (1488–1524) A military leader, Olid commanded one of the three Spanish armies during the final assault on Tenochtitlan. In 1522 Olid led an expedition to Honduras and tried to establish his own rule there. He was accused of rebellion and executed.

BERNARDINO DE SAHAGÚN (CA. 1499–1590) Sahagún came to Mexico as a missionary in 1529. He devoted his life to learning about the history, language, and culture of the Mexica people. The results of his painstaking research were collected in the *Florentine Codex*, perhaps the most valuable source of information on the world of the Mexica.

GONZALO DE SANDOVAL (CA. 1498–1529) A loyal companion of Cortés, Sandoval commanded one of the three armies that attacked Tenochtitlan in 1521. He went to Spain with Cortés in 1528 and died there. According to reports, the gold that Sandoval brought from Mexico was stolen while he was on his deathbed.

DIEGO VELÁSQUEZ (1465–1524) Velásquez came to the New World with Columbus on his second voyage in 1493. He conquered the island of Cuba and became its first governor in 1511. Velásquez sent out two expeditions (1517 and 1518) to explore the coast of Mexico. In 1519 he planned a third expedition with Hernán Cortés as its leader, but he soon had reason to regret his choice. Velásquez opposed Cortés's actions throughout his time in Mexico and tried, unsuccessfully, to have him captured and returned to Cuba.

SOURCE NOTES

4 Fernando de Alvarado
Tezozomoc, *Crónica
Mexicayotl,* in Miguel Leon-
Portilla, *Pre-Columbian
Literatures of Mexico*
(Norman: University of
Oklahoma Press, 1986), 117.

9 Bernardino de Sahagún,
*General History of the Things
of New Spain,* trans. Arthur
J. O. Anderson and Charles
E. Dibble, bk. 10 (Santa Fe:
School of American Research
and the University of Utah,
1950–1982), 196.

10 Ibid.

17 Ibid., 70.

18 Ibid., 9: 5

21 Ibid., 2:84–85

12 Ibid., 10: 165–69.

28 Christopher Columbus, *The
Log of Christopher Columbus,*
trans. Robert H. Fuson
(Camden, ME: International
Marine Publishing, 1992), 51.

31 Ibid.

34 Ibid., 76.

34 Ibid., 75.

35 Ibid., 77–78.

35 Ibid., 85.

35 Ibid., 76.

35 Ibid., 77.

35 Ibid.

36 Francisco López de
Gómara, *Cortés: The
Life of the Conqueror by
His Secretary,* trans. and
ed. Lesley Byrd Simpson
(Berkeley: University of
California Press, 1964),
8, 9.

37 Ibid., 8.

41 Ibid., 22.

43 Bernal Díaz del Castillo,
*The Discovery and
Conquest of Mexico,*
trans. A. P. Maudslay
(Cambridge, MA: Perseus
Book Group, 2003), 26.

43 Ibid., 25.

45 Díaz del Castillo, 32.

45 López de Gómara, 19.

45–46 Ibid.

39 Bartolomé de Las Casas,
*A Short Account of
the Destruction of the
Indies,* ed. and trans.
Nigel Griffin (London:
Penguin Books, 1992),
13.

48 Hernán Cortés, *Hernán
Cortés: Letters from
Mexico,* trans. and ed.

Anthony Pagden (New Haven, CT: Yale University Press, 1986), 50.

49 Díaz Del Castillo, 54.

51 Ibid., 67.

52 Ibid., 71.

52 Ibid.

52 Ibid., 72.

53 *Florentine Codex*, in Stuart B. Schwartz, ed., *Victors and Vanquished: Spanish and Nahua Views of the Conquest of Mexico* (Boston: Bedford/ St. Martin's, 2000) 31.

56 Díaz del Castillo, 74.

56 Ibid., 75.

57 Cortés, 27.

58 López de Gómara, 74.

58 Ibid., 108.

58 Cortés, 51.

59 Díaz del Castillo, 122.

60 Ibid., 130.

60 Ibid.

61 Ibid., 132.

61 Ibid., 143.

62 Cortés, 67.

62 Ibid., 154.

62 Ibid.

63 Cortés, 73.

63 Díaz del Castillo, 179.

64 *Florentine Codex*, in Schwartz, 121.

64 Díaz del Castillo, 179.

64 Ibid., 186.

65 *Florentine Codex*, in Schwartz, 121.

65 Ibid., 192.

66 *Cantares Mexicanos*, in Leon-Portilla, *Pre-Columbian Literatures of Mexico*, 87.

66–67 Díaz del Castillo, 193.

67 *Florentine Codex*, in Miguel Leon-Portilla, *The Broken Spears: The Aztec Account of the Conquest of Mexico* (Boston: Beacon Press, 2006), 64.

69 Cortés, 101, 102, 106.

69 Díaz del Castillo, 216.

69 Ibid., 219–220.

70 Ibid., 220–221.

70 Ibid., 204.

70–71 Cortés, 88.

73 Díaz del Castillo, 297.

74 López de Gómara, 208.

74 *Florentine Codex*, in Schwartz, 163–164.

74 Ibid., 164–65.

75 *Florentine Codex*, in

Leon-Portilla, *Broken Spears*, 72.

76 Díaz del Castillo, 297.

77 Ibid., 309–310.

77 *Fernando de Alva Ixtlilxochitl*, in Leon-Portilla, *Broken Spears*, 90

78 Díaz del Castillo, 312, 313.

78 Ibid., 313.

79 *Florentine Codex*, in Schwartz, 180.

80 Ibid.

81 Díaz del Castillo, 317.

82 López de Gómara, 240.

84 *Florentine Codex* in Leon-Portilla, *Broken Spears*, 93.

86 Ibid., 336–337.

86 Díaz del Castillo, 337.

87 Ibid., 337–338.

88 López de Gómara, 240–241.

89 Díaz del Castillo, 344.

90 Ibid., 388.

92 *Cantares Mexicanos*, in Leon-Portilla, *Pre-Columbian Literatures of Mexico*, 87.

93 Díaz del Castillo, 353.

93 López de Gómara, 262.

93 Díaz del Castillo, 392.

94 Ibid., 393.

95 Ibid., 399.

95–96 Ibid.

96 *Florentine Codex*, in Leon-Portilla, *Broken Spears*, 96–97.

98 Ibid., 96.

99 Díaz del Castillo, 416.

101 López de Gómara, 270.

101 *Florentine Codex*, in Leon-Portilla, Broken *Spears*, 97–98.

101 Ibid., 98.

102 Ibid., 99.

104 Cortés, 239.

105 Díaz del Castillo, 436.

105 Ibid., 137.

105 *Florentine Codex*, in Leon-Portilla, *Broken Spears*, 107.

107 Ibid., 109.

107 Cortés, 223.

107 *Florentine Codex*, in Leon-Portilla, *Broken Spears*, 109.

108 Díaz del Castillo, 443–444.

108 *Florentine Codex*, in Leon-Portilla, *Broken Spears*, 109.

108 Ibid., 112–113.

108–109 Ibid.

110 López de Gómara, 292.

110 *Florentine Codex*, in Leon-Portilla, *Broken Spears*, 118.

111 López de Gómara, 296.

111 *Cantares Mexicanos*, in Leon-Portilla, *Broken Spears*, 137–138.

112 Cortés, 158.

113 López de Gómara, 323.

118 Cortés, 332.

118 López de Gómara, 331–332.

120 Cristóbal Pérez, quoted in Hugh Thomas, *Conquest: Montezuma, Cortés, and the Fall of Old Mexico* (New York: Simon and Schuster Paperbacks, 1993), 585.

121 López de Gómara, 349.

122 Ibid., 356.

122 Ibid., 390.

122–123 Ibid.

124 Ibid., 404.

124 Ibid., 407.

125 Ibid., 408.

125 Ibid., 409.

126 Schwartz, 1.

127 Ross Hassig, *Mexico and the Spanish Conquest* (Norman: University of Oklahoma Press, 2006), 193.

128 Schwartz, 214.

129 Alvarado Tezozomoc, *Crónica Mexicayotl*, in Leon-Portilla, *Pre-Columbian Literatures of Mexico*, 117.

SELECTED BIBLIOGRAPHY

PRIMARY SOURCES

Columbus, Christopher. *The Log of Christopher Columbus*. Translated by Robert H. Fuson. Camden, ME: International Marine Publishing, 1992.

Cortés, Hernán. *Letters from Mexico*. Translated and edited by Anthony Pagden. New Haven, CT: Yale University Press, 1986.

Díaz del Castillo, Bernal. *The Discovery and Conquest of Mexico*. Translated by A. P. Maudslay. Cambridge, MA: Perseus Book Group, 2003.

Fuentes, Patricia. *The Conquistadors: First-Person Accounts of the Conquest of Mexico*. Norman: University of Oklahoma Press, 1993.

Leon-Portilla, Miguel. *The Broken Spears: The Aztec Account of the Conquest of Mexico*. Boston: Beacon Press, 2006.

López de Gómara, Francisco. *Cortés: The Life of the Conqueror by His Secretary*. Translated and edited by Lesley Byrd Simpson. Berkeley: University of California Press, 1964.

Sahagún, Bernardino de. *General History of the Things of New Spain*. Translated by Arthur J. O. Anderson and Charles E. Dibble. Santa Fe: School of American Research and the University of Utah, 1950–1982.

Schwartz, Stuart, ed. *Victors and Vanquished: Spanish and Nahua Views of the Conquest of Mexico*. Boston: Bedford/St. Martin's, 2000.

SECONDARY SOURCES

Aveni, Anthony. *Empires of Time: Calendars, Clocks, and Cultures*. Boulder: University Press of Colorado, 2002.

Berdan, Frances F., and Patricia Ruff Anawalt, eds. *The Codex Mendoza*. Berkeley: University of California Press, 1992.

Bierhorst, John, ed. *The Hungry Woman: Myths and Legends of the Aztecs*. New York: William Morrow and Co., 1984.

Carr, Raymond, ed. *Spain: A History*. New York: Oxford University Press, 2001.

Carrasco, David. *City of Sacrifice: The Aztec Empire and the Role of Violence in Civilization*. Boston: Beacon Press, 1999.

———. *Daily Life of the Aztecs: People of the Sun and Earth*. Westport, CT: Greenwood Press, 1998.

Chavero, Alfredo. *El Lienzo de Tlaxcala: Explicasión de Las Laminás*. Mexico City: Editorial Cosmos, 1979.

Clendinnen, Inga. *Aztecs: An Interpretation*. Cambridge: Cambridge University Press, 1995.

———. "Fierce and Unnatural Cruelty: Cortés and the Conquest of Mexico." *Representations* 33 (Winter 1991): 65–100.

Davies, Nigel. *The Aztec Empire: The Toltec Resurgence*. Norman: University of Oklahoma Press, 1987.

Duran, Diego. *The Aztecs, the History of the Indies of New Spain*. Translated by Doris Heyden and Fernando Horcasitas. New York: Orion Press, 1964.

Hassig, Ross. *Aztec Warfare: Imperial Expansion and Political Control*. Norman: University of Oklahoma Press, 1988.

———. *Mexico and the Spanish Conquest*. Norman: University of Oklahoma Press, 2006.

Lanyon, Anna. *The New World of Martín Cortés*. Cambridge, MA: Da Capo Press, 2004.

Las Casas, Bartolomé de. *A Short History of the Destruction of the Indies*. Edited and translated by Nigel Griffin. London: Penguin Books, 1992.

Leon-Portilla, Miguel. *The Aztec Image of Self and Society*. Translated and edited by Jorge Klor de Alva. Salt Lake City: University of Utah Press, 1992.

———. *Aztec Thought and Culture*. Translated by Jack Emory Davis. Norman: University of Oklahoma Press, 1963.

———. *Fifteen Poets of the Aztec World*. Norman: University of Oklahoma Press, 1992.

———. *Pre-Columbian Literatures of Mexico*. Norman: University of Oklahoma Press, 1986.

Moctezuma, Eduardo Matos. *Treasures of the Great Temple*. La Jolla, CA: ALTI Publications, 1990.

Pierson, Peter. *The History of Spain*. Westport, CT: Greenwood Press, 1999.

Schroder, Susan, Stephanie Wood, and Robert Haskett, eds. *Indian Women of Early Mexico*. Norman: University of Oklahoma Press, 1997.

Serrato-Combe, Antonio. *The Aztec Templo Mayor: A Visualization*. Salt Lake City: University of Utah Press, 2001.

Soustelle, Jacques. *Daily Life of the Aztecs*. Translated from French by Patrick O'Brian. Mineola, NY: Dover Publications, 2002.

Thomas, Hugh. *Conquest: Montezuma, Cortés, and the Fall of Old Mexico*. New York: Simon and Schuster Paperbacks, 1993.

FURTHER READING AND WEBSITES

BOOKS

Ackroyd, Peter. *Cities of Blood*. New York: DK Publishing, 2004.

Childress, Diana. *Barefoot Conquistador*. Minneapolis: Twenty-First Century Books, 2008.

Hamilton, Janice. *Mexico in Pictures*. Minneapolis: Twenty-First Century Books, 2003.

Jolley, Dan. *The Smoking Mountain: The Story of Popocatépetl (An Aztec Legend)*. Minneapolis: Graphic Universe, 2009.

Lanyon, Anna. *Malinche's Conquest*. Saint Leonards, Australia: Allen & Unwin, 1999.

———. *The New World of Martín Cortés*. Cambridge, MA: Da Capo Press, 2004.

Leon-Portilla, Miguel. *The Broken Spears: The Aztec Account of the Conquest of Mexico*. Boston: Beacon Press, 2006.

Platt, Richard. *Aztecs: The Fall of the Aztec Capital*. New York: DK Publishing, 1999.

Saunders, Nicholas, and Tony Allan. *The Aztec Empire*. Chicago: Heinemann Library, 2005.

Smith, Jeremy. *The Aztecs*. Milwaukee: Gareth-Stevens Publishing, 2005.

Sonneborn, Liz. *The Ancient Aztecs*. New York: Franklin Watts, 2005.

Stein, R. Conrad. *The Story of Mexico: Cortés and the Spanish Conquest*. Greensboro, NC: Morgan Reynolds Publishing, 2008.

WEBSITES

Ancient Middle America: Aztecs, Nahuatl, Tenochtitlan. http://www.d.umn .edu/cla/faculty/troufs/anth3618/maaztec.html#title. This website contains information useful to students, including bibliographies of books and DVDs and links to other sources of information.

The Aztecs/Mexica. http://www.indians.org/welker/aztecs.htm. This website includes information on the Mexica language, gods and myths, the calendar, and many other subjects.

Museo de Templo Mayor. http://archaeology.asu.edu/tm/index2.php. This website, created by the Mexican government, describes the excavated ruins of the Great Temple in Mexico City and the associated museum.

Reinterpreting Malinche. http://userwww.sfsu.edu/~epf/2000/jt.html. This article discusses the different interpretations of Malinche's role in the Spanish conquest and the view modern Mexicans have of her.

Spanish and Nahuatl Views on Smallpox and Demographic Catastrophe in the Conquest of Mexico. http://www.hist.umn.edu/~rmccaa/vircatas/vir6 .htm. This article examines the smallpox epidemics that struck Mexico in the 1500s and discusses the role they played in the Spanish conquest.

Teaching and Learning: The Conquest of Mexico. http://www.historians.org/tl/ lessonplans/ca/fitch. This site, developed by a professor of history, contains much valuable information, including biographies of major figures and side-by-side comparisons of Mexica and Spanish source material.

vgsbooks.com. http://www.vgsbooks.com. Visit vgsbooks.com, the homepage of the Visual Geography Series®. The "Mexico" page provides links to useful on-line information about Mexico, including geographical, historical, and cultural websites.

INDEX

ABOUT THE AUTHOR

Sylvia A. Johnson is an award-winning writer and editor of nonfiction books for young readers. She has a special interest in the history and culture of ancient Mexico. Sylvia has toured ancient Mexican cities such as Palenque, Uxmal, and Teotihuacan. She has also studied Mexica art and culture in the extensive collection of the Anthropological Museum in Mexico City. To learn more about the cultures of Mexico, she has even taken courses in reading the hieroglyphic writing of the ancient Maya. Sylvia makes her home in Minneapolis, Minnesota.

PHOTO ACKNOWLEDGMENTS

The images in this book are used with the permission of: The Granger Collection, New York, p. 5; The Art Archive/Mireille Vautier, p. 11; © Newberry Library/SuperStock, p. 13; The Art Archive/Museo Ciudad Mexico/Gianni Dagli Orti, p. 15; The Art Archive/Museo del Templo Mayor Mexico/Gianni Dagli Orti, p. 19; The Art Archive/Templo Mayor Library Mexico/Gianni Dagli Orti, pp. 20, 75, 116; Library of Congress (LC-USZC4-743), p. 26; The Art Archive/Real Monasterio del Escorial Spain/Gianni Dagli Orti, p. 31; © Laura Westlund/Independent Picture Service, p. 38; © North Wind Picture Archives, p. 40; The Art Archive/Museo de America Madrid/Gianni Dagli Orti, pp. 42, 46; © Diego Duran/The Bridgeman Art Library/Getty Images, p. 51; The Art Archive/Biblioteca Nacional Madrid/Gianni Dagli Orti, pp. 53, 60; © Roger-Viollet/The Image Works, p. 55; © The British Library/HIP/The Image Works, p. 68; The Art Archive/Museo Colonial Antigua Guatemala/Gianni Dagli Orti, p. 73; © Spanish School/The Bridgeman Art Library/Getty Images, pp. 77, 109; © Foundation for the Advancement of Mesoamerican Studies, Inc., www.famsi.org, pp. 84, 106; © age fotostock/SuperStock, p. 88; © SuperStock, Inc./SuperStock, p. 99; The Art Archive/Antochiw Collection Mexico/Mireille Vautier, pp. 100, 136; © Image Asset Management Ltd./SuperStock, p. 104; The Art Archive/Museo Ciudad Mexico/Gianni Dagli Orti, p. 113; The Art Archive, p. 119; The Art Archive/Gianni Dagli Orti, p. 129.

Cover: © akg-images.